THE KNACK OF SELLING

TEN STEPS TO SELLING THE AUSTRALIAN WAY

MAT HARRINGTON

CONTENTS

ABOUT THE AUTHOR

Mathew Harrington has over 26 years of experience as a sales representative with a number of companies, mainly in the electrical wholesale industry, and has worked in both capital city and country environments.

While in high school, Mathew worked at both McDonald's and KFC, both positions giving him the foundation of a strong work ethic. Working as a waiter from age 18 also proved a great environment for learning customer-service skills.

His career in the electrical wholesale industry began in a storeperson role, from which he worked his way through various positions with leading wholesalers and manufacturers, until taking on his current role as a sales representative with a family-owned Australian company.

One of his greatest career highlights was being awarded sales representative of the year twice while working for one of the largest companies in the electrical industry, which led to once-in-a-lifetime experiences of travel to South Africa and Hong Kong.

Mathew is still very passionate in his role as a sales representative today and is always seeking new and different ways to deal with customers in a rapidly changing environment.

In February 2019, Mathew was again awarded sales representative of the year for a third time, this time with his current employer.

INTRODUCTION

This book is a must-read for anyone in sales or thinking about getting into sales especially in a face-to-face environment.

If you're already working in sales, you'll find practical advice that you can put into action on the job to improve your performance. If you're considering applying for a sales position, you'll find invaluable tips that can help you present some ideas to a potential employer in an interview.

A big thanks to Scott Pape, the Barefoot Investor: if I hadn't read his book and taken *action*, none of this would have happened.

As Pape says in *The Barefoot Investor*, you need to "bring home the bacon". This book will help you do just that. By taking *action*, following the ten steps described in this book, you will be able to confidently apply for a job in sales or develop in your existing sales role.

This book is designed to be read multiple times, just like a movie that you might watch again and again. Coming back to it, you will pick up on parts that you missed the first time around. Only by reading the book, highlighting the relevant points that apply to you specifically, and taking action to implement the steps in your real-life sales experience will you get the best results.

It may take time to get through it all and take action, but make it happen—you won't look back!

Purpose

My purpose in writing this book was to share the experience and knowledge I've gathered over 26 years of work experience, to educate prospective salespeople, as well as people already in sales roles, no matter their industry.

I realised there are currently few books by Australian authors that go into detail about the face-to-face selling process and all that goes with it.

Honestly and truthfully sharing my experiences and what I've learned, here I've put my sales mind on paper for the first time.

Early in my career, I was thrown the keys to the company car and expected to work out how to sell for myself with no training or experience—absolutely nothing! But I worked it out, and because of that, this book can give future sales representatives a head start towards getting the results their employer is chasing.

Each of the ten steps I describe for you here has its own

section dedicated to retail selling, because in these environments customers come to you. This is distinct from many sales roles, where you have to go to the customer, and often have to find those customers for yourself.

I also discuss what I consider one of the most important aspects of selling—cold calling. Most sales representatives find cold calling difficult, but it's vital that you learn this skill, which brings in new customers and results in business growth.

Is selling an art?

Selling is absolutely an art. Just like mastering any art form, perfecting the skills involved in selling takes time and effort.

This book will take you through what I believe are the ten vital steps that will help you master the knack of selling.

Getting a sale can be very satisfying.

Getting a regular customer can be very satisfying.

But growing a business, keeping staff in jobs, creating more jobs and employing more staff is the ultimate reward.

A career in sales carries a lot of responsibility and entails a lot of hard work, but if you are successful, the rewards are very much worth it.

Success doesn't come to you—*you go get it!*

Customer-service basics

The customer is the lifeblood of one's business and must be looked after in the right way.

The way you greet a customer, either in person or on the phone, is crucial to continued sales. First, you must always maintain a smile, and second, you must convey a happy persona regardless of how you actually feel. Always begin by greeting the customer with a positive attitude.

Not every day will be a good day for you personally, but you must always be happy on the outside and communicate with your customer in a way that makes them feel happy too. If you can achieve this, and as long as your product or service is great, you will have some loyal customers who will continue to come back.

Recently, I attended a dinner with some colleagues at a popular restaurant in town, which has a great reputation for Thai food.

After arriving and being shown to our table and given menus in an almost empty restaurant, we sat down and started chatting. Ten minutes passed, we still had no drinks on the table, and not a soul had spoken to us.

The initial impression is one of the most important things in selling; it is the first verbal or physical communication that sets the tone, as well as your presentation. And in the above example, by not attending to our table, the restaurant left an impression that its customer service was not very good. Though the food was great, all we think about now when discussing the restaurant is that poor service.

This restaurant reduced the likelihood of repeat sales with us due to bad customer service. Worse, we are also likely to tell other people about our bad experience, which may make them think twice about going there.

Word of mouth is one of the cheapest forms of advertising. When used positively, word of mouth can increase sales, but, conversely, it can also reduce sales when the word is bad.

Later in this book, in step 5, there is a section that talks about complaints and how to handle them. Complaints must be dealt with immediately and professionally to reduce the likelihood that they will progress to a negative outcome.

Think about your local milk bar or coffee shop. If you're a regular or even semi-regular customer, the people that work there will usually know your name and your most frequent order. That gives the transaction a personal touch, encouraging you to return, as you feel welcome and it's an enjoyable place to go.

Whatever industry you choose to grow your sales career in, always get to know your customers well and understand what they prefer to buy.

Why face-to-face when the internet is taking over the world?

People love to interact with each other in a context where

it's fun or rewarding, and business transactions are built on trust and relationships made through such interactions over time. That's one reason why face-to-face sales is still so important.

Buyers also consider warranties: although they may be offered online, there is security in being able to head into the store you bought from and instantly sort out an issue.

People also often use the internet to check prices, and then head to where they are most comfortable buying from and negotiate on the price from there. This is merely part of the sales process.

The internet will no doubt continue to take some business from the traditional market, but there will always be a role for salespeople in many industries and markets.

Customers want confirmation that they are making the right buying decision. The role of the salesperson is to confirm this and make the decision for them, which they can most readily do in person.

Customers often want to touch and feel what they are going to buy. This is also part of confirming they are making the right decision, and it can *only* be done in a face-to-face environment.

Now, let's get into the ten steps that make up *The Knack of Selling*.

Read on!

STEP 1: PREPARE AND PLAN

The importance of preparation and planning

Before you do anything in life, you must prepare and plan for it. If you don't, you are almost guaranteed to fail. Nothing is more important in sales than preparation and planning.

The time it takes to prepare and plan may seem significant, but you must realise it's not a waste of your time. It's a very important part of being a very successful salesperson, and is as crucial to bringing home the bacon as is finding new customers and making sales calls.

A typical week for a sales representative will involve four days of sales calls and one day of preparation and planning, which includes any follow-up required from the four days of sales calls.

It is important to always allow the day for follow-up. If you don't, you will find yourself bogged down because you've created too much work for yourself and don't have enough time to complete it. This will affect your customer service, as you will find that your response times in getting back to your customers will grow, negatively affecting your prospective sales.

In saying this, people employed in sales roles will often be able to delegate some tasks to internal sales staff (see "Internal and External Sales Staff" in step 6 for an explanation of this distinction). In a typical year, you will be limited in the amount of time you have to conduct physical sales calls, due to things like holidays, sick leave and training, and delegating is one of the only ways you can get beyond this limit to multiply your productivity.

Here is an estimate of the number of actual selling days you may have to conduct face-to-face sales calls each year:

- 52 weeks per year (52)
- less 2 weeks of public holidays (50)
- less 4 weeks annual leave (46)
- less 1 week of sick leave (45)
- less 2 weeks of travelling time (43)

That gives you 43 weeks of actual face-to-face selling time, or 172 days based on four days selling and one day of follow-up each week.

If you are not organised, you will have even less time.

Therefore, it is imperative that you prepare and plan for each week as best you can, so all your time is used productively and you ensure you get the best sales results possible.

When planning your calls, I suggest that you always have a backup plan.

Generally, a day will never go as planned, even if you organise it to the best of your ability. A customer may postpone a meeting, there could be some sort of emergency, or another customer may call you with an urgent matter that you have to address before you can get back to your planned day.

I recommend that you always have some extra calls or quotes to follow up on at any time during the week. I personally kept a folder with all my "things to do" in it, so I could take care of them any time I was free during the day due to a call or meeting not going ahead. Later in my career, the customer relationship management (CRM) system supplied by my employer replaced my folder: I discuss this technology later in the book.

Preparation and planning for sales is a bit like what you do when cooking. Before you can cook anything, you need to get all the ingredients together, you need to make sure you have all the equipment to put the ingredients in, and then you need to spend the time doing the actual cooking to achieve the desired result: a dish to eat.

Sales is very similar: the ingredients could be the sales tools (sales folder, products, agenda), the equipment could be the call planning, and the actual sales call is what you need to spend time doing to create the desired dish of a sale or follow-up.

Research

Before attending an interview for a sales position, always review the website of the company you propose to join. Understand their business as much as you can from the information on their website. Before they ask you, let them know that you understand a little bit about their business. This will definitely put you in a good position with the interviewer. In the interviews I have taken part in myself as an employer and as a potential employee , this alone has generally resulted in a second interview and a job offer.

Then, as a salesperson, understand your customer. Today, information is readily available, and as part of your preparation, you should research as much as you can about your prospective customers (known as *prospects*). Google now gives us a chance to do this very easily. The Yellow Pages (not so much their hard copy anymore, but their website) can also provide valuable information as a starting point. You may also have business associates or partners (for example, supplier representatives) who can give you information about potential customers in your market. Get as much information from as many sources as you can find.

Use the information you discover to your advantage. For example, if the business you are researching has an outstanding website, then when you first make contact, be sure to tell the customer that you've noted their excellent presence on the internet. They have probably spent a considerable amount of time and money developing their website, and will appreciate that you've made the effort to examine it.

Want to learn more about research?
I've developed a training video at
knackofselling.com.au/members.
Join today to take a look at this video and others.

Another example of something you could note is that a business may have diversified into several areas within their chosen industry. They may have spent a lot of time and money on training and licences to achieve this. For example, one electrician may just do domestic work and nothing else, while another may offer a variety of services, including domestic electrical work and CCTV (closed-circuit television, or camera installations). This makes them different from the other electricians in their market and will no doubt result in them getting more work. In talking to a prospect like this, you can comment on how they are different to the average company within their industry, and suggest there may be a way your company can sell a product or offer a service that relates to a range of their own offers. You might also see an opportunity for your company to get into a new market to service the customer.

The website of a potential customer will often identify the

main contact of the business and their email address. You can then ask for them by name, which will often get you past the gatekeeper and straight to your contact. Follow up your call with an email afterwards.

Today, social media can also give you further information. Check Facebook and LinkedIn to find out more about your contact and their interests, looking for things you have in common that you could talk about in your sales call.

My suggestion is to gather as much information as you can about the business you wish to contact. Put this information in bullet form and have it in front of you when you make that first phone call.

As a salesperson, if you can identify and keep track of the unique opportunities each prospect presents, develop a marketing strategy that addresses those opportunities (usually in consultation with your internal marketing department), implement it and get some sales, you will be well regarded by senior management. Adjusting to capture new opportunities is often how companies diversify themselves and keep up with market trends and changing customer bases. It all starts by listening to the customer.

Product knowledge

For a car salesman, preparation and planning includes learning about every vehicle on their lot in detail, both used cars and new. When a potential customer walks onto the lot, the questions they ask are the key to working out which of these cars to show.

The same process applies for any other kind of sales. You have to know what cars are on your lot: what products or services you have to sell. And you also have to understand them in detail so you can communicate their merits to buyers. If you don't know what you have, or can't work out what the potential customer wants, chances are you won't show them what they're looking for, and you will lose the sale.

Whatever you are selling, make sure you fully understand it.

Get your knowledge from the internet

Today, there are YouTube videos on most products. Watching these can be a great way to get more knowledge about a product you don't yet understand thoroughly. In some cases, you can even see the product being installed, which can be very helpful.

Typically, you can also look up pricing on the product if you are unsure what your competitor is charging. The customer may have done similar research and be aware of the price they expect to pay, so your knowledge will help if this comes up during the transaction.

Get your knowledge from customers

If you know a customer well enough, you can put the product in their hands and get their opinion on it. Do this with a couple of customers, and you will be able to use that knowledge with any future customers.

As an example from the electrical industry, when I received a new product to sell, I would first research it by getting all the information I could from the supplier, especially their sales representative. From there, I would call up a great friend who worked in the industry as an electrician, and put the product in his hand to get his opinion. In some cases, I would let him install it and get his feedback. Then, when making a sales call on an actual customer (another electrician), I could use the knowledge I'd gathered. This showed I knew my stuff, and always helped in achieving a sale.

Also understand the business you work for in detail, as you may have to sell the business first before you sell a physical product. This is particularly important for customers who might be looking for a consistent supply of a component for their own products, or who will need ongoing support for what they buy from you. These customers want to know your business is trustworthy, reliable and will be around for the long term.

Some things you may want to know about your business are:

- its history
- points of difference from its competitors (not always price)
- any activities or organisations it sponsors in the community

- what experience its employees have

Get your knowledge from suppliers within your industry

Supplier sales representatives can be a great source of information, but these days, most suppliers also have great websites that communicate relevant product information.

Get your knowledge from industry groups

Groups devoted to particular industries or products can often be found on Facebook and LinkedIn, and joining them can be a valuable source of information.

Before commencing any sort of promotion or special, it can be useful to do a quick survey of a range of customers to see if you can get an idea of what the take-up will be like, or some suggestions to improve the promotion. Industry or product-focused groups on social media can be a source of survey participants, and you can use the knowledge you gain to your advantage. Sales will likely follow.

As an example, a co-worker of mine recently decided to put together a special pack of tools for new electrical apprentices. Before deciding on what to put in the pack, she surveyed potential customers to determine the list of tools. This survey resulted in the pack containing the tools most likely to be used by electrical apprentices, and the sales effort benefited.

Let co-workers extend the limits of your knowledge

You have your own knowledge and skills, and these have their limits. But you can use your co-workers' knowledge and skills to your advantage to make a sale.

Within the business you represent, there will often be a number of employees, all with knowledge and skills in different areas. Your task as a salesperson is to understand what knowledge and skills each person has and, depending on your customer's question, to get the answer from the right staff member.

Knowledge is everything: make sure you have plenty of it!

A note on cold calling

In my current role, the senior management of the company I work for put a challenge to me to go into a new market where most potential customers had no idea about the business I represented. My task was to open some accounts and start some sales transactions, in the knowledge that the company would open a new branch in this market in 12–18 months.

As part of my preparation and planning, I developed a cold call information folder that contained everything relevant about our business, including how we do things differently from our competitors. The aim was to use this in a face-to-face cold call, if given the opportunity, and hand it to the potential client after going through it with them.

The cold call information folder guided me during the call and removed any fear I may have had of not remembering everything important to discuss. I had everything right in front of me. This gave me great confidence and, as I completed more and more cold calls, presenting the material became natural to me.

As the account application form was reasonably extensive to fill out, I prefilled all the information I could get from the potential customer's website. This not only saved time but also showed the potential customer I had gathered some information and was interested in their business.

Make it a priority to put together your own cold call information folder for the business you work for or are looking to start working for. Most businesses will have a marketing department, and contacting them is a great place to start looking for information. You should also contact any suppliers you have, and get some flyers as well as any product samples they may have available.

I will discuss cold calling in more detail in the next few chapters, and explain how my challenge panned out.

Want to see what a cold call information folder contains?
I've developed a training video at
knackofselling.com.au/members.
Join today and take a look at this video and others.

Retail therapy: The "sales call"

In a retail environment, preparation and planning is a little different to what a salesperson would do for a face-to-face sales call. There are similarities, though—while a sales representative's car is their office and showroom, in a retail environment, the showroom is the masterpiece.

The first part of your preparation should be to make your store look and feel inviting. You should do whatever it takes to present your business in this manner.

A cleaning roster should be in place for all staff to follow, to make sure the showroom is pristine at all times. Think of it like this: if you go to a restaurant and the toilets are dirty and your meal comes out on a dirty plate, you may never go back there. Customers visiting a dirty or disorganised showroom may have the same reaction.

The second part is to make sure all your stock is in the correct area and has the applicable price on it. Shelves should be full and the stock pulled to the front.

Your displays should be in prominent positions. In some cases, your suppliers will pay to be in these prominent positions, as there is more chance of their product selling and being restocked.

Ensuring your showroom is fully stocked and well presented is the best preparation you can do in a retail environment.

Presentations

Before any presentation, you should always prepare the room you will be presenting in. Make sure it is clean and there is plenty of water available. Every attendee should be given a pad to write on and a pen. I always put a few bowls of Mentos on the table, as they seem to disappear —people must enjoy them.

If you have any guest speakers, make sure their equipment and any audio or video needed works in the presentation room, before the presentation begins. Ask guest speakers to arrive half an hour early so they are ready to go on time.

If there is any information you want the attendees to receive, have it prepared beforehand. Ask your presenters to bring any flyers or giveaways with them, and have them ready before your presentation begins.

Before beginning your presentation, practice this breathing technique to calm yourself and put you in a more relaxed state:

> *Deep breath in…*
> *Exhale.*
> *Deep breath in…*
> *Exhale.*
> *Deep breath in…*
> *Exhale.*

Always keep a glass or bottle of water near where you are

presenting, as taking a sip can be a great way to clear your throat and will also buy you some time to relax if you're nervous.

Step 1 summary

Prepare and plan. Take the time to prepare and plan for the week ahead. Make sure you are organised.

Research. Spend the time to research and gain knowledge.

Knowledge. Knowledge is everything. Make sure you have plenty of it!

A note on cold calling. Prepare and plan for your cold calls. Make up a cold call information folder that contains everything about the company you represent.

Retail therapy. Keep your showroom fully stocked and well presented.

Presentations. Organise the room where the presentation is going to take place, check all equipment and make sure that it works with your presenters' equipment.

STEP 2: PRACTICE AND PRIOR LEARNING

Practice and prior learning

Once you've prepared and planned for your sales calls, the next crucial step is to practice. This is something you will have to do continually throughout your sales career to develop yourself.

There are a few ways to practice. You could do so alone by yourself in front of a mirror, or with a friend or another sales representative role-playing as your prospective client. If you have a close friend that is also a customer, and you can explain to them what you are trying to achieve, you might also do a practice sales call with them.

Another great idea is to offer your services free to a business that you are looking to get a sales role in, or a business in an industry you are interested in. Ask if you can spend some time with the existing sales staff to watch and learn as much as you can. This will represent prior learning for future study or work. You can relate it back to the marketing course you will enrol in later, using it as an assignment to gather real-life sales experience before taking on a sales role.

If you are currently in a full-time job but not in sales, I suggest that you offer to do work experience and gain some prior learning on a Saturday (if the business is trading) to gain some sales experience within your chosen industry.

I often hear stories of people who did this and got a job offer from the place where they volunteered, because they fit into the business so well. This may not happen straight away, but some time down the track, it is a distinct possibility. By doing the hard yards early, you reap the rewards later.

If you really want a sales role, don't stop at one work experience prospect—try many! Offer your services to many businesses in many different industries. You just never know what will float your boat—or theirs.

In fact, I would strongly suggest that, if possible, you spend some time with other sales representatives in your company, especially out on the road when they are doing actual calls on customers. You will find that people do things differently, but there will always be some similarities, and spending time on the job with others will be a valuable learning experience.

Attend any after-hours business functions, trade shows and so on that you are invited to. Mingle with everyone there, and gather as much information as possible from the stands at trade shows.

If you are in a sales role and have an industry trade event coming up, make sure you invite your customers along. Meet up and have a drink beforehand; make them feel like you have gone out of your way to get them to the event.

If your business has a branch or outlet, allocate some time in your week to spend there if it's possible. It is important that internal sales staff who work in the branch or outlet all day feel you are a part of the team, and you may also teach them a thing or two while you go about your business internally. Deal with some customers and ask some open-ended questions; you will learn a lot from this exercise. Listen to how the other staff and management interact with the customers. As the external sales person, it is important to ensure that all the staff in the branch or outlet understand that you are also contributing to the overall goals of the team, even though you are not in the branch or outlet much of the time due to your role.

Role-play with fellow employees can prove invaluable and will often improve how you go about your sales calls. Although role plays can seem daunting, they helped me tremendously, especially the suggestions I got from other staff.

With the cold call information folder you made in the

previous chapter, ask another staff member to sit down and act as the customer. Explain the details to them; for example, they might play a prospective customer who knows nothing about the business. Act out the call with them as though it was a real-life, face-to-face sales call.

Turn practice into habits. For example, practice answering the phone as follows:

> Hello, and thank you for calling (business name). How can we help you today?

The more you practice your set response when answering the phone, the more it will become a habit. Others you work with will often pick up on your habit and follow suit.

In team meetings, practice marketing strategies before putting them into action, so the team understands. In doing so, you will ensure the team knows what steps to follow when they deal with customers.

As an external sales representative, make sure you are aware of all your business's current marketing initiatives. Understand the components of each promotion before going to the market with them. Marketing will often come up with some great promotions, but the sales representative needs to do some work to make sure it is presented or delivered to the customer seamlessly.

The advice regarding pre-filling account forms also

applies to promotions. If any forms have to be filled out, pre-fill as much of them as you can before attending the physical sales call. The same goes for registering on an app: ask the customer for their phone and fill out the information on their behalf.

Training

Contact your local technical college (TAFE) and ask about relevant courses that are available. A marketing course or a business course can be a good beginning to a career in sales.

From my own experience, enrolling and making the commitment to yourself that you will succeed in a course is a great start. Mind you, it took me a lot of hard work after hours to get through my certificate IV in business (marketing). At one point I nearly gave up, but thanks to my wife, I succeeded, as she pushed me to get it done.

From the day I started to the day that I finished, I applied the principles I learned in my role at the time as an external sales representative. It was valuable for the growth of my sales career, and I have not looked back. The course in marketing has a direct link with sales, so I started to think outside the box, developed my own marketing ideas and strategies, and implemented them in the workplace.

If your employer offers training at any stage throughout your sales career, you should always put your hand up.

Even if it is for something you may have touched on in the past, it does not matter. Any training is good training, and it will show your employer that you want to develop yourself personally and benefit their business.

I strongly suggest that you invest in *you*; you will develop yourself personally and be able to contribute a lot more in your sales role. This should be an ongoing commitment that you make to yourself throughout your whole sales career.

The training videos on my website can be a great place to start to deepen your experience of the steps in my book. See **knackofselling.com.au/members**.

There is no excuse for not making a commitment of this kind. But if you feel you are unable to follow through, consider trying this strategy:

Tell a good friend you know who will hold up their end of a bargain that if you commit to a course of your choice, you will give them $1,000 to deposit into their account. Every week that you attend, you will receive a percentage of the $1,000 back, until you receive your completion certificate. Tell the friend that should you pull out of the course, you will have forfeited the funds and they can have one hell of a party at your expense.

If this incentive doesn't float your boat, think of something that will, then work hard to complete the training to get that incentive.

A note on cold calling

As mentioned under the heading "Practice and Prior Learning", I conducted a number of role plays where I would go through the cold call information folder with fellow staff to prepare me for my upcoming cold calls. This practice made it so much easier for me when I actually made my first cold call.

I also practised the initial phone call with colleagues, and made dot-point notes that proved very helpful when I actually made that first phone call. I also made notes as I made further real-life calls. The same subjects would often be brought up, and my notes gave me easy access to the answers.

Make practice happen in your workplace!

As much as you may dislike role-playing, I guarantee that doing it even a few times with different people will give you invaluable experience that will make the actual initial phone call or sales call a lot easier.

Retail therapy: Practice and prior learning

In the retail environment, practice is very important, especially when it comes to current sales catalogues.

You should know everything that's in your current catalogue, as this will often be the attraction to customers coming into your store. Practice will involve studying the catalogue front to back, along with all types of media, including television, social-media and print adverts.

Ensure you have enough stock of the advertised products and that you have them displayed in a prominent position. You should also understand your competitors' current sales catalogues, so that should a customer ask if you can offer a similar deal, you'll be right on top of it.

I was recently impressed with a retail store when I called in to purchase an item that I usually get from that particular store. I asked if they could match a competitor's price that I saw elsewhere, and the salesperson got onto their computer to confirm I was correct.

In this case, the competitor's promotion had concluded, but the salesperson told me that she could still give me a 20% discount for being a loyal customer to their store. She then also gave me a 20% discount voucher for my next purchase.

This process has guaranteed another sale, made me feel good about the store for matching the competitor's price, and made me feel good again about knowing that I'm going to get another 20% off a future purchase.

Presentations

After putting together a slideshow presentation, always get someone (usually your partner or a work colleague) to check every slide for punctuation, grammar and content.

Then practice reading the content aloud to make sure

you're all over it. Add notes to the bottom of each slide so that you can see what slide is coming up next while presenting.

It is also a good idea to have handouts prepared for attendees.

After having spent a lot of time practising presentations, I have found that by doing this and having a full understanding of everything I will talk about, I can make myself less nervous than normal when actually presenting.

It is also important to clarify with the audience that they understand the content and message you are giving out. "Does that make sense?" is always a good prompt to the audience to get this clarification every couple of slides.

Step 2 summary

Practice and prior learning. Practice on a regular basis throughout your sales career.

Training. Make it a goal to enrol in a course this year. Always accept any offer of training from your employer, even if it is a refresher.

A note on cold calling. Role-playing customer interactions with a colleague can prove to be very beneficial.

Retail therapy. Know your business's sales catalogues and advertising back to front.

Presentations. Practice your presentation aloud multiple times before you present.

STEP 3: MAKE INITIAL CONTACT

It's all about confidence

You have completed your preparation and planning, and practised how your initial contact with the customer might go. By doing this, you have already built up some confidence.

The next step is to make that phone call.

In step 1, you wrote down some dot points to guide you in the conversation. You have around 10–20 seconds to get the person's attention. Your objective should be to get an appointment for a face-to-face meeting. At worst, you could aim to get their email address so you can start the communication flowing via email.

Communication is everything in sales, as you will soon learn.

Hang on a minute.

Read the next section, on rejection, just in case you get rejected on that first call. Make the call once you have completed reading all of step 3.

Rejection and objection

In the search for the perfect woman, I was rejected many times, with things such as, "I've already got a boyfriend," or a slap in the face. I really had no chance in these circumstances; this was definitely rejection at its finest.

What do you think I did with all this rejection? I soldiered on and never gave up. That's exactly the attitude you need to have as a salesperson.

Rejection can damage many people's confidence. However, it should be taken as a learning experience that can have a very positive outcome. Also, in some cases, the rejection is actually an *objection*, and you should learn to recognise this.

Rejection and objection can take many forms, and it is important that you identify the type of rejection or objection you have received to turn it into a positive outcome.

The first type of rejection is what I call *extreme rejection*.

This can hurt your confidence the most. An example: You make a phone call, introduce yourself quickly and the business you are representing, and get told to "nick off" in an angry voice. You might also hear something like, "I'm not interested in the stuff you're offering!" or, "I'm very happy with my current supplier, and I have no interest in changing; don't waste my time!"

It is very important that you never give up. I don't mean you should give them another call. I mean you should make a note about the incident, as they may become a customer of yours in the future for whatever reason. Then disregard the conversation and move onto your next prospect. You won't get extreme rejection from most prospects; normally it's just an occasional few. If you do happen to get a few extreme rejections in a row, take some time out, take a deep breath and continue. Remember, *never give up.*

The next type of rejection is called *time-poor rejection.* This type of rejection is very common, and does not mean the potential customer does not want to see you. In fact, this is more an objection than a rejection. Often, in business, you may contact a potential customer at the wrong time, and the response to your conversation may go something like, "I'm sorry, but I don't have time right now. I am very busy, goodbye."

Alternatively, you may have to leave a voicemail message on their mobile, as they could be busy and unable to answer your call.

The best way to handle this objection is, if you have their email address, send a quick email stating that you spoke to them or left a message on their mobile, and ask for a suitable time, place and date for a meeting in a few weeks' time. If they have an office, but you don't have their email address, call the receptionist and ask for it.

Should you get no response, another call a few weeks later may get a better response. It may also be that you don't know the customer very well. There is normally always a time in every customer's day, whether it is very early in the morning, late afternoon or possibly nearer to the end of the workday, when they may have some time to talk to you.

With some clients, you may even be able to catch them for a frothy at the pub after work!

Once again, the receptionist at a customer's office may know this type of information, and in the next step, I have included a topic on relations with receptionists and admin staff.

The next type of rejection is *no-value rejection*: "I don't like sales representatives as they waste my time, and I'm happy dealing with the staff in the store." The customer doesn't see any value that you can offer. The challenge here is to be able find something of value for this customer at some stage in the future.

It is very important to respect the customer's wish. However, the same customer may always be grateful for a quick phone call to say, "Thank you for your business!"

You should be armed with some information before calling the customer to thank them. For example, how long have they been trading with your business, and what are their payment terms and monthly spend?

The phone call could go something like this:

> Hello, Mr Jones, it's Mat Harrington here from *Knack of Selling*. This is just a quick call to say thank you for your business, as a customer who spends $2,000 per month with us and also pays their account within 30 days, you are very important to us. If there is anything we can help you with, please give me a call. I also have some information on the latest new product to hit the market. Can I email you some information?

Always end the conversation with a question so that you hopefully get the response you are chasing.

This conversation makes the customer feel good and respected, and even though he does not physically want to see you, you still manage to get the information to him via email. You just never know—he may give you a call and place an order for the latest new product at some stage.

Another type of rejection, which is more related to a face-to-face sales call, is *order rejection*. Our response to this is called *handling the no*.

Order rejection happens when you have fully conducted your sales call (following all the steps in steps 4, 5 and 6 of this book), and at the conclusion of the call, you ask for the order and the customer tells you they do not want to place it.

Some customers need time before they make their decision. Never get upset by this rejection, as in most cases it is an objection. First, the product may be something application-specific, and the customer will order it when the application comes up. It may also be that the customer just needs to take in all the information and a follow-up a few days later may result in a sale.

Sales is all about relationships. When a customer says no at the beginning, it doesn't mean he will never purchase anything from you. In fact, the first call opens the communication channel and is the beginning of the business relationship.

Walk away from a face-to-face meeting with confidence, knowing that the customer was willing to let you visit them and to hear your offer.

Make and confirm your appointments

One of the most important things in this step of making initial contact is to make and confirm an appointment with the customer.

There are four key principles to follow, if possible, within your first phone call.

1. Offer the prospect something that will save them time.

2. Offer the prospect something that will make them money.
3. Offer the prospect something free as an incentive to buy.
4. Whatever you offer the prospect, make sure it is simple to obtain. If it will take a lot of time, the prospect likely will not do it.

Then, make a *day*, a *time* and a *location* for your face-to-face meeting.

After you have agreed on the details, you must send a simple email to the customer as confirmation. Then, on the morning of the proposed meeting, it is vital that you make a quick phone call to reconfirm the appointment.

As an example, I recently introduced a new, younger sales rep to an existing customer. I did all the preparation work, organised the appointment for a Monday, and then the Friday before, I confirmed the appointment by phone.

Then, when the actual Monday came around, I handed over the reins to the younger sales rep. The manager of our branch suggested to the younger sales rep that they contact the customer before we leave, to confirm the appointment and also to see if the customer needed us to bring some products to them.

The customer's first response was that if we hadn't contacted them, they would most likely have forgotten the appointment, as they'd had a big weekend drinking beer and had forgotten about Friday's phone call.

The second response was that they needed some products as well, so we got a sale! The younger sales rep learned a vital lesson, and was very excited to get the sale.

Another example regarding appointment confirmation involves a physical store. During my career as a supplier representative, I had a lot of stores to call on, and the habit that I developed—which proved to help me become very successful—was simply to call before I came.

It is common for other sales representatives just to rock up unannounced and then attempt to make a sale. In most cases, they would politely be told to leave.

I often called the manager of the store, first because they were an important decision-maker, and second because they would then give me some time in person, or advise of a more suitable time or another staff member to see.

I always met with the manager but also made sure I spent time with all the staff. More often than not, a manager is only as good as their staff.

I got the most important things done first—any returns of products, faulty or otherwise, and resolving any issues with transactions I was conducting with the business at the time. Then I would always have a new product or promotion to discuss.

When I was the manager of a store myself, I was amazed at the number of sales representatives who did not call ahead. It was unprofessional, and such a simple thing can make a big difference.

As a supplier representative, over time my relationship with a store manager would develop, and they would often tell me it was not necessary to call them beforehand. I still did, as this was how I operated, and there would always be times when the customer was short-staffed or just too busy to see me. At those times, they appreciated the phone call and happily rescheduled the appointment.

A note on cold calling

The points raised in the first topic in this step, "It's All About Confidence", are just as applicable to a physical cold call, where you have not even made an appointment and the opportunity appears out of nowhere. For example, you might be driving along and you see a tradie's van that you don't recognise on a job site.

During my career, I have called on tradesmen randomly with no notice many times. In all these cases, the tradesmen were unknown to me, and represented a new opportunity.

These calls were just to gather information in preparation for starting the sales-call process. Luckily, as I recommended you do in step 1, I had made up many cold call information folders and always had spares with me. When I came across a random opportunity to do a cold call, these were very handy.

I would always make sure that I got the potential customer's business card with their details on it as an outcome from the cold call.

In cases where I couldn't track down the person but located their work vehicle in the street, I would leave my business card under their windscreen wiper or in the driver's-side window seal, hoping they would give me a call when they returned to their vehicle.

In some cases, the recipient of the card would call me, but where they didn't and I had their contact details from signage on their vehicle, I would follow up the next day to make sure they got my card.

Retail therapy: Initial contact

In retail, the initial contact with a customer is more likely to be in the form of a catalogue in the mail, an advertisement on television or even a Facebook post.

That initial contact—the advertisement—then steers the consumer into the physical store or inspires them to make a phone call.

If you are prepared and know your sale catalogues, as discussed in step 2, then your initial contact will be positive.

Always have copies of your current sales catalogues handy so that when a customer asks you a question, you can refer to it as a reference, whether in-store or on the phone.

Sometimes, sales catalogues may require you to write the part numbers relevant to the actual product on them, as they only have the name of the product and not the sales code. Always keep a master copy with this information on it.

Step 3 summary

It's all about confidence. Communication is everything in sales, so start communicating—make the initial contact.

Rejection and objection. Know the difference between rejection and objection, and know how to handle rejection and turn it into a positive outcome.

Confirm your appointments. Make the appointment and confirm it. This is crucial to get to step 5: attending the physical sales call.

A note on cold calling. Sometimes, opportunities to cold call customers come around unexpectedly. Armed with your cold call information folder from step 1, you will be ready. Keep spare cold call information folders on you.

Retail therapy. Keep copies of current sales catalogues in the store to review with customers.

Now, take a deep breath and make the call!

STEP 4: CRUCIAL THINGS TO
CONSIDER FOR YOUR SALES CALL

Punctuality

When you confirmed your appointment in step 3, you made a time to meet the customer, and it is vitally important that you keep to this time. For most people in business, time is money, and there is nothing worse than wasting a customer's time. You will lose all respect from them, and it will be a long road back. There is always a competitor waiting for that moment when a customer's preferred supplier slips up for whatever reason.

At a recent sales conference I attended, one regional sales manager spoke about an example of punctuality that I will never forget—and neither will he or the manager that went on the sales call with him.

The manager of a branch arranged an appointment on a particular day with one of his top clients, in conjunction with his regional sales manager. The regional sales manager turned up at the store ready to go out around an hour before the confirmed appointment time. The manager continued working and getting tasks done, and it wasn't until the regional sales manager made him aware that their appointment was in 20 minutes that he finished up what he was doing. They then jumped in the car and headed to the appointment, which they arrived at 20 minutes late due to traffic. On entering the customer's workplace, the regional sales manager noticed straight away that the customer was not happy. The customer allowed them some time, but basically brushed them off. He was very busy that day, and his schedule did not allow him to adjust his day for them.

Going forward, the manager found that his relationship with the customer changed. Sales declined, and he knew he would have to put in a lot of effort to get the customer's sales back.

Never be late to an appointment or, if you experience a genuine issue that makes it impossible for you to arrive on time, make a phone call and speak to the customer directly. Do not text unless they do not answer.

Punctuality can also apply to returning a phone call. You may be busy and unable to answer, and the customer may leave a message on your voicemail to return their call. The absolute worst-case scenario is that you don't call him back, in which case you should not be in a sales position. An acceptable scenario is that you call him back at least by the end of the day; however, I would always call back at my first available opportunity, and this would often be within two hours. If you follow this principle, you will be seen as professional and interested in your customer, and your sales will invariably increase.

Email has now become one of the main communication channels in the sales process, and punctuality also applies here. Sometimes, emails can be overwhelming, and it is very important that you filter and prioritise them to highlight the most important ones. Delete any that are junk, and remember to unsubscribe from any that are irrelevant to prevent them reappearing.

These days, it is commonplace to get emails on your mobile, and this has definitely improved response times. However, it is vitally important that you don't get bogged down in emails. Later in the book, I discuss time management, and deal with emails in more detail.

The main thing to do when you receive an email is to reply with an acknowledgement that you have received it and will take action in due course.

It could be as simple as this auto-reply:

> Hello, and thank you for your email,
>
> I will read your message and respond at my next possible opportunity, at worst by the end of business today. If it is urgent, please don't hesitate to give me a call on my mobile.

If no action is required, and the email is from a reputable

source, a reply with thanks to the name of the person who sent it will at least acknowledge that you received it.

Attitude

Attitude is everything, and can have a massive impact on a business in terms of repeat sales. As a salesperson, never give a customer the impression that you have a bad attitude—in fact, it is better you stay home rather than bring it to work. A lot of hard work has gone into getting the customer to deal with you and the business you represent. This can all be undone extremely quickly with a bad attitude.

Some ways to get rid of a bad attitude include playing your favourite music, taking some time out at your favourite coffee shop, giving a close friend a call or going out and smelling the roses! Just make sure that attitude is gone pronto, before you even think about dealing with any customers.

I remember one Friday night happily going into my local bottle shop, grabbing my favourite beverage and heading to the counter. The salesperson at the counter failed to acknowledge me, scanned my box of coldies and said, "That's $48, mate," in an angry voice. I paid the money and left. The salesperson's attitude made me feel less happy than when I walked in.

I visited a different bottle shop the next Friday, where I was greeted at the door and asked if I needed assistance. I grabbed my coldies and went to the counter. There was the salesperson, who, with a big smile on their face, offered me the $10 special (a $20 bottle of red for half price) since I'd already spent the $48, then happily took my money and said, "Have a great evening."

I now go there regularly and often accept the upsell special.

Smile, tell jokes, be happy and offer your customer a coffee! Coffee often puts the customer in a relaxed place where they will be more open with you when you ask open-ended questions.

Attitude is everything.

Attitude results in more sales.

Personal presentation

The way you present yourself directly reflects the business you work for, and in a sales role, you are normally the first point of contact. It is vitally important that you maintain your appearance to a high standard. Personally, I always polish my shoes every morning, iron my pants and shirt, and generally make sure that I look clean-cut and professional. You will never succeed in sales without your presentation being A1.

If your employer does not give you a uniform, you will have to invest in some clothing and shoes. This investment will pay itself off tenfold and should be something you make a priority.

Vehicle presentation

In most sales representative roles, you will be allocated a company car as a part of your package. Your vehicle will become your office and, like a physical office in a building, you should keep your workspace in order.

Think about the last time you visited someone's office and it was very clean. Maybe there were trays with documents, labelled "inbox", "outbox", and "action". The desk area was free of documents, and it felt inviting to come in and sit down to discuss business and do a deal.

An office like this looks organised and gives the impression that any business discussed will be dealt with in an efficient and orderly manner. Your vehicle is no different. It needs to be well organised and kept clean and respectable, inside and out.

You never know when a manager of your company or a customer may hop in your vehicle for various reasons, and their first impression will determine how they view you and the business you represent.

Listening

The common saying in sales is that salespeople talk too much and don't listen.

Let me tell you that it is very important to talk while in a sales call, but listening is much more important!

You should ask open-ended questions and listen for the

answer, as it is often in the answer that a sales opportunity will come about. If you aren't listening, you won't hear the opportunity and therefore won't make a sale.

Let me give you some examples:

New vehicle sales representative: What do like about the new Toyota Corolla hybrid you have been looking over?

Customer: I like the fuel efficiency, but not so much the look. I really like the new Hilux, and I think if I can convince the other half that they have similar fuel efficiency, I might get what I'm really after.

By asking an open-ended question first and listening to the answer, the sales rep here can tell that the customer is after a different style of vehicle but with good fuel efficiency. The turbo diesel now offers this, and the rep can offer what the customer is really after. As they know all the vehicles in the lot, they should know that there may be an in-between option that can satisfy both parties— the customer and their other half.

There is nothing worse than walking into a store, branch or car lot and not being asked any questions. The customer is obviously there for a reason, and as a salesperson, we need to ask open-ended questions to find the sales opportunity. Never forget this.

Have a specific agenda

An agenda is one of the most important things to have ready for a sales call.

You may have already prepared a cold call information folder with all the details about your business, or a sales folder with relevant promotions and product flyers. This is great, but a specific agenda to tick off is also a great thing to have.

I wrote an agenda for each meeting in the space in my diary for that day, which I would take into the sales call and refer to regularly to make sure I discussed all the necessary topics.

I always discussed items from that specific agenda first before bringing the cold call information or sales folder into the equation.

As an example, some specific topics from an agenda could include:

- Thank the customer for their business, discuss the numbers and let the customer know how important they are to your business.
- Discuss any staff changes relevant to the customer.
- Address an issue the customer has raised.
- Discuss current sales promotions (sales folder).
- Finish with a CTA (call to action).

Want to see how to make an agenda?
I've developed a training video at
knackofselling.com.au/members.
Join today and take a look at this video and others.

Mobile-phone etiquette

The customer's mobile or office phone is often the lifeblood of their business; so if a customer's phone rang during a sales call, I would always tell them to answer if they needed to.

My mobile, on the other hand, is different. I would always put my mobile into silent mode and in my trouser pocket before calling on a customer. This is being respectful to the customer, as their time they are giving you is valuable and if you answer a call while you are with them, they will not feel very important.

I would only take my tablet into a sales call for two reasons:

1. To access the CRM and review a customer's numbers with them.
2. To show any presentations I may have.

Nowadays, you can get your mobile to show who is calling on your smart watch. Though this can be distracting, it can be handy. For example, if your wife is due to have a baby and she calls you, this would be an acceptable excuse to answer the call. Having said that, though, I would normally raise the possibility at the start of the sales call so the customer understands the urgency to answer.

Step 4 summary

Punctuality. Never be late to an appointment. If you are going to be late for whatever reason, make sure you call the customer directly and speak with them.

Attitude. Don't bring your bad attitude to work. Leave it at your front door!

Personal and vehicle presentation. Presentation is everything; make sure it is A1!

Listening. Ask lots of open-ended questions.

Have a specific agenda. Different customers will need certain things discussed that are relevant only to them. Write these down and address them in the sales call.

Mobile-phone etiquette. Always put your mobile on silent before going into a sales call.

STEP 5: ATTENDING THE PHYSICAL SALES CALL

Receptionists and administration

Most businesses have a receptionist, and they are a very important person in the sales process.

Often, the receptionist is the one who pays the bills. They have valuable information that can clarify how you are travelling with the customer, if you can get them to share it with you.

Here are a couple of recent examples.

I called into a customer's office to drop off the remainder of the goods from a recent sales order. Knowing my regular contact wouldn't be there, I decided to find out where the business I represent sat in relation to the customer's overall purchases.

On entering, I greeted the receptionist by name. Always

keep a note of the receptionist's name in your customer's file.

I explained to the receptionist that I was calling to drop off some goods and that I usually spoke to her boss. I then asked if our statements had been coming through efficiently, and she said they had. I asked if she had any issues with the company I represented, and she replied that no, they didn't. I then asked her where the company I represented sat in terms of purchases made over a month, in her opinion and with the knowledge she had.

She told me the business she worked for had four main suppliers and that the business I represented sat third out of four in terms of dollars spent.

This information clarified to me that I still had a lot of work to do with the customer, and that my challenge was to improve our position over time.

In another example, after calling at a customer's premises for a while and struggling to get some serious face-to-face time with the key person, the receptionist politely told me that the person I was chasing played golf every second Friday afternoon, and that this would be the best time to catch him.

In fact, she said she would tell him that the company I represented had paid for his next golf game and that I looked forward to meeting him then.

This turned out to be the best golf game I ever played … from a business point of view!

This customer became a regular buyer, and we met up at least once a quarter for a game of golf to keep developing our relationship.

You should always maintain a great relationship with the receptionist. In fact, you should aim to be well known by all of the management and staff within a business if possible.

In a small business, the spouse or partner is often "the receptionist" and will work from a home office. The best way to start developing a relationship with them is to make contact about a subject relevant to their role, such as account payment or signing up to a website. It is also advisable to get them to some functions, which will help them understand your business better and give you the chance to start developing a professional relationship with them.

If both parties are talking about you, your chances of sales success increase.

Handling complaints

Sometimes in a sales call, before you even get to the point of trying to sell something, you may get a complaint from your customer.

My first question in a sales call is to ask my customer if they have had any issues, as if they did and you address those issues first and come up with a solution, it proves to them that you back up what you are selling. This process is extremely important, as then, when the customer is forced to choose between two suppliers, the chance of them picking you is greater. They know that should anything go wrong, you will take action and find a suitable solution, which reduces their risk.

An example of bad complaint handling is realising that something has happened, normally due to reduced sales, and then not doing anything about it. A lot of people are afraid to address issues, but this is something you must learn to deal with.

I was recently challenged with the task of getting a customer back to dealing with the company I represented. Sales to them had declined dramatically, and no action had been taken to address "the issue". The manager knew "the issue", but for whatever reason—probably fear of facing the customer—never addressed it.

The first thing I did when meeting with the customer was to address "the issue". Put simply, I explained that whatever happened in the past, if we could put that behind us, make sure there was a measure in place to ensure it never happened again, and move forward, that would be great.

He respected me for bringing up "the issue" and offering a solution, and we carried on with business from that day forward. This customer is now one of the branch's top ten customers, and I enjoy going there every week. In fact, we have developed a very strong business relationship over time, which has resulted in sales increasing to the point where he is now in the business's top five customers.

Sometimes you may come across a customer who vents his anger at you.

I can recall a number of examples in my career, and I will share a couple with you.

The first happened very recently, when I called a customer while training a new representative who also knew them, to follow up on a quote. The customer was made aware he was speaking to us both, and after that, he proceeded to explain to me in a strong voice that he would come into our branch on his own and I was not to hassle him. I responded in agreement with him and remained totally calm. I thanked him for his time and hung up.

The new representative met the customer at a later date, and the customer told him, "I was a bit hard on Mat the other day." The new representative could see he felt guilty for saying the wrong thing.

Guilt like this can be used to get a sale in future; you can gently remind the customer of what happened and make them feel how they made you feel.

In the second example, a customer made one of our internal sales staff cry when he rang the office and spoke with her. I was in the office at the time, and when she hung up, I asked her what was said. The customer had sworn at her and said some bad things. They were totally out of line.

I went straight down to the customer and addressed the

issue, simply stating that no one should be spoken to as he had, especially in a professional environment. We appreciated his business, but this was not acceptable.

He apologised and immediately rang the office to apologise directly to the staff member.

Always deal with complaints and issues straight away. Try to find a solution, remain calm and use your normal voice. Never lower yourself to the level of the person complaining, or who is in the wrong. If you do and you start an argument, you will never see the end of it!

Calculating margin

This section is extremely important when calculating the price at which you sell to your client. You may already know how to do this effectively, or you may not.

First, imagine you buy a product for $55.00, and wish to make a margin of 20% when you sell it to your customer.

Many people will grab a calculator and simply add 20% to $55.00, which will give you $66.00. Try it now. Did you end up with $66.00?

In fact, this is not a true 20% margin, and you are short-changing yourself and the business you work for.

The true way to add margin is to deduct whatever percentage you wish to add from 100, and then use division.

Here are a couple of examples:

First, let's do the same calculation as above: you wish to add 20% to $55.00.

100 less 20 equals 80. You then *divide* $55.00 by 0.80 to get the correct answer.

$55 ÷.80 = $68.75.

Let's say you made 1,000 sales of this particular product.

The incorrect way ($55 + 20%, multiplied by 1,000) results in $66,000.

The correct way ($55 ÷ 0.80, multiplied by 1,000) results in $68,750.

This gives you an extra $2,750 in revenue. Now imagine your business has 5,000 products in its portfolio and you apply this principle when selling them all. The benefit is enormous.

If you take nothing else from this book, make sure you understand this calculation method and use it. Even better, explain it to your superiors. Even if they know it, they will be impressed with you, as they will know that you are adding profit to the bottom line and have good business sense.

Here is one more example, just to make sure you are on the same planet…

You wish to add 32.5% to your cost of $77.50.

100 less 32.5 equals 67.5.

$77.50 divided by 0.675 equals $114.81.

Always remember to round the final number up as well.

Negotiation

Negotiation is essential in any sales call. Just like a marriage, there needs to be a bit of give and take from both parties.

We have just discussed margin calculation. It is important that you understand your margin so that you understand how far you can move, to avoid giving away your entire margin.

Negotiation can take many forms: price reduction, offering something for free, giving an incentive, etc. If the customer is new, sometimes you can take a hit on your margin, expecting the customer will be happy with your offer and you will get repeat business. Once you have established a great relationship and shown you can offer great service, you can often add a bit more margin to your sales.

Often in sales, the customer only remembers the mistakes you make and not the times you provided exceptional service and bent over backwards for them. It is not often you get a thank you, especially when you are in a service industry.

The best satisfaction a salesperson can get is to review their account and look at the sales and margin. In some cases, just an individual sale itself is enough. When you have a tough negotiator as a customer, it is quite rewarding when you review their account or just a single sale and see that they are still very profitable for your business.

Negotiation can also take place when your business buys goods from suppliers to offer to your customers. You may sometimes be able to negotiate a better buying price and even to get the supplier to help with the cost of marketing their product.

In fact, I know some salespeople who bank on the fact that if they discount their product to get the sale, their supplier will be able to compensate them with a better buying price. Rather than take this risk, it is far better to contact the supplier first to make sure they are giving the best price. The mention of a competitor often results in a reduced cost.

Remember, your supplier wants your sale just as much as you want your customer's.

Apply negotiation to your everyday life. Think about your utility bills, insurance and mortgage. Google the best deal for your current supplier and make sure you are getting it. If not, call them and make sure you get it.

Upselling and cross-selling

Very early in my career, I was working two jobs, one as a storeperson at an electrical wholesaler, and the other as a bottle-shop attendant. In the bottle shop, there was always the chance for both an upsell and a cross-sell all in the one transaction.

A customer would come into the bottle shop and ask for a six-pack of beer. If I told them they would be better off with a slab, as they were on special, they would often take up the offer.

Then I would present Smith's crisps to them on a two-for-one offer, and this was often taken up, though not all the time.

Upselling and cross-selling is a great way to add value to your existing client base, which is more cost-effective for a business than acquiring new customers.

The topic of upselling was briefly touched on in the "Attitude" section of chapter 4, when I discussed the poor service I received at one bottle shop. At the second shop I tried, the customer service was fantastic, and the salesperson presented an upsell that I took them up on.

Often, in a retail environment, the upsell and cross-sell products are located conveniently on or close to the sales counter. Look around next time you are in a convenience store, supermarket or pet store. Think of a time when you got home and thought, "Did I really need that?"

Think of the chocolates and lollies at the counter of a service station. The attendant will always ask you if you are interested.

Think of a lighting shop with the globes for all the light fittings. One for each fitting is obviously a necessity, but why not keep a spare? The attendant may remind you of this.

Think of a newsagent that keeps footy cards on the counter. These have cost me a fortune—my kids would always ask if they could have a pack, and then, of course, the folder to go with them.

Upsell or cross-sell products are normally of a similar or lesser value than the originally purchased product, but not always.

It could also be that you discuss one particular product as the purpose of your face-to-face sales call, and then discuss your whole offer as the upsell.

If you think of something along the lines of "this goes with that", this is often all you need to present to the customer to make an upsell.

Your management will be impressed if they see you offering upsells to your customers. Furthermore, locating the right products to upsell is another great initiative. If other staff see you being successful and selling more, they will often follow suit.

Products and flyers

In any face-to-face sales call, it is important to always have something to put into your customer's hands. This gives them some responsibility to listen, and to look at and touch what you are discussing with them.

This can include not only products but also promotional items, for example, a jacket or beanie. Give the jacket or beanie to the customer to try on. Tell them they look good in it, or how warm it will keep their head.

The thing you give them may also be an app. Ask for the customer's phone, download the app, and register the customer for it while you have the phone in your hand.

The same applies to any form that coincides with a promotion. As discussed in the "Practice and Prior Learning" section of step 2, fill out as much as you can yourself and then ask the customer to complete the rest.

This method even works when applied to an account-opening form, as we have also discussed earlier in the book. When you hand a form to the customer with some of their details already filled out, it makes them feel obliged to finish it.

The likelihood of getting a sale increases if you are proactive in getting the item in the customer's hand or on their body, or in pre-filling forms.

Always have a sales folder that includes flyers and specials. The sales folder has proved to be an exceptional tool for me, as it can serve as a guide to what needs to be spoken about in the sales meeting. It ensures that nothing will be forgotten. However, time management does come into play, as you need to recognise if the customer has the time to discuss everything you have to present.

The best way to manage your time in presenting the

contents of your sales folder is to organise it so the important topics are at the front and the not-so-important ones at the back. This way, if you don't get through everything, you have covered the crucial points and can discuss the remaining topics on the next sales call.

If you contact a customer and they are unavailable, I would always recommend that you mention that you will email them or drop the latest flyer on the newest available product into their letterbox.

Hopefully, the customer will read what you send them. If not, it still creates something for you to follow up on in the next sales call, possibly with an actual sample of the product in the customer's hand.

Want some extra pointers on how to set up your sales folder?
I've developed a training video at
knackofselling.com.au/members.
Join today and take a look at this video and others.

Loss-leader products

Loss-leader products are very important in sales; they attract the customer to your branch or outlet. Loss-leader products are those often sold at below cost, with the expectation that the customer will buy other goods whose margin makes up for what is lost in selling the loss-leader. This method is used in many industries to attract new customers.

Here are a couple of examples.

In a supermarket, milk is a loss-leader product. However, to encourage extra sales, milk is placed at the back of the supermarket, which banks on you buying other products you pass on your way in or out.

In an electrical wholesale branch, the electrical cable used for power and lighting in domestic applications is a loss-leader product. It is normally placed at the back of the branch, and more often than not is used to entice customers to place orders including other products that boast a higher margin, counterbalancing the negative margin on the loss-leader.

The pitfall can be that you attract a new customer by offering a loss-leader, but in the next few sales the service is not up to scratch and the customer goes back to their original supplier. Then, you may not recover what was lost in selling the loss-leader.

In the section of step 6 covering internal and external staff, you will see that if internal staff are not briefed on having to give a new customer exceptional service, everything can fall apart pretty quickly.

In fact, service should be exceptional for all customers. This is how businesses become very successful and then very profitable.

The product life cycle

Every product has a life cycle. Just as people are born, live for a time and then die, so does a product. In fact, some products become loss-leaders towards the end of their life cycle, but eventually, most will be replaced with newer versions.

This is why we continually see new products come onto the market, to replace older ones. Older products see price reductions as they mature, while new products command a higher price.

The product life cycle is what keeps the market moving. Businesses make heavy investments in research and development to keep new products coming out.

As a salesperson, it is important that we recognise where the product we are selling sits in the life cycle. This helps us to determine:

- the selling price
- what new technology will replace it

For example, in the electrical industry, there has been a rapid change in what lighting is used in a domestic setting. Look around your house, and most likely all your globes will now use LEDs (light-emitting diodes). This technology replaced the older incandescent bulbs, including halogens.

When halogen was around the peak of its popularity ten

years ago, the price was around $50 per light; five years ago it was $25 per light and LED technology was starting to evolve.

Now, halogen is pretty much extinct, and LEDs can be had at a very competitive price.

If an electrical business didn't recognise this shift to the new LED technology, it would be stuck with stock that it could not sell. It is very important to continually review your product range in line with market trends and adjust accordingly.

Adjusting does two things: it shows your customers you are ahead of the game, and reduces your chances of having stock you cannot sell.

Sales opportunities with good margins are born from new technology; make sure that, whatever industry you work in, you are ahead of the game. Continually do your research and use it to your advantage.

Keep abreast of any regulation changes in your industry, and always try to be one of the first to discuss these with your customer. This will let the customer know you are a fountain of knowledge, and going forward, they may often call you with questions that can result in sales.

I would suggest keeping up with the trends in whatever you are selling or going to sell. Join relevant groups on Facebook and LinkedIn, read magazines and spend some time gathering information from websites.

A note on cold calling

As discussed previously, I attended physical cold calls after lots of role-play practice, and was armed with my cold call information folder that I would go through during the call and leave with the potential client.

These calls aimed to get the prospect to open an account. As this was the last subject in the folder I had prepared, if possible, we would fill the form out on the spot. As discussed earlier, I pre-filled these forms with information I gathered from the customer's website before the call.

I had a business card with all my details in the folder. Should the customer not have enough time to fill out the form on the spot, I would lock in a day and time the following week to pick it up from them.

The day before my confirmed appointment the next week, I would also give them a quick call as a reminder to fill it out before I got to them the following day.

My results speak for themselves. Remember, we had no physical presence as an electrical wholesaler in this market, but the business was going to open a branch serving it within the next 12–18 months.

I opened 50 accounts within 12 months, and made more than $130,000 in sales to those accounts in the same time.

This work created a great footprint for the new business and a great head start as it was getting into a new market.

It created a sense of security for new staff, and certainly added to the excitement of getting sales for the team from our new customer accounts.

It is important you pump yourself up before you attend a cold call. Play your favourite song loud to get your blood pumping; this will give you extra confidence.

Remember that in the sales call, if you feel you need to take notes, make sure you ask the customer their permission, as sometimes it can be seen as rude.

You may also need to take another staff member with you for various reasons. Having two staff members together lets you bounce off each other and get through the cold call easier. You must have a reason for the second staff member being there. For example, you might present them as a specialist in an area you know the customer is interested in.

Cold calling on customers is a skill all employers will rate highly, as it means new customers, more sales and more profit.

If you can succeed in cold calling, you will become a valuable asset to your employer. This will enable you to negotiate the best pay.

Preparation and practice are crucial in getting the confidence up to conduct your first cold call. If it fails, you know how to handle rejection, then move onto the next one.

I think of cold calling like fishing. You make a phone call, and often you will have to leave a message. If they ring back, you've got a live one and a real chance to get in front of them, since they called you back to hear more about what you have to offer. If you communicate with them immediately and get a meeting, you've also hooked a live one.

When you are in front of the prospect, if you achieve your objective, which in my case was to get an account form filled out, then you've caught the fish!

Whenever a new customer signs up, I always set up a meeting at the branch for them to meet with all the staff and view the stock to get the ball rolling.

Now—go fishing and hook a few big ones! I look forward to hearing about them when you reach step 10.

Retail therapy: Physical sales calls

In retail, generally you don't attend a physical sales call; the physical sale comes to you.

It's the marketing that generally makes the process happen. As discussed in steps 2 and 3, some customers will come into the store after seeing some of your marketing material in various media. Others will come in to browse, but you know they have an interest in something you sell. Your task is to find out what this is, and that's the challenge.

Never judge a book by its cover!

There were a number of times during my career where a customer presented themselves, and after one look, I assumed there was no way they would spend much.

Of course, I was wrong, and in one case, the transaction was quite significant. It is very important that you give all customers the same service, regardless of their appearance.

The first essential thing to do is to greet the customer.

Secondly, just like in a face-to-face sales call, open-ended questions are essential to obtaining the right information. You should ask a lot of these questions.

Closing a sale in the retail environment is best done while the customer is in your store. Often, if they leave, they will not return.

At worst, get the customer's contact details so you can email them some information after they leave. If you give them a brochure or catalogue to take with them, make sure your store's contact details are on them.

Your customer service needs to be A1, and you must ask the customer if they need any help or are looking for something in particular.

Tap and go etiquette

With the introduction of new tap and go payment technology for credit and debit cards, there is some etiquette involved before tapping a customer's card, as I have learned.

While I was completing a transaction recently, the customer handed me her card and without any thought I tapped it over the EFTPOS machine. I handed her card back, she asked what I did, and I said I had tapped the card and it all went through.

She then got upset and explained that I should have asked her if it was okay to tap before doing it. She prefers to insert the card and use her PIN, as in her thinking that's more secure.

I told the story to a colleague and she said she had experienced the same thing with a different customer.

The lesson is: when doing transactions with credit and debit cards, if the value is under $100 and you could use tap and go, always ask the customer if it is okay first. Or simply make it a habit to ask the customer "tap or insert" and let them tell you what they want to do.

Step 5 summary

Receptionists and administration. Make sure you develop a business relationship with the receptionist and all key staff if possible.

Handling complaints. Remain calm; use your normal voice and behaviour.

Margin calculation. Remember the margin calculation formula.

Negotiation. It's give and take. Consider offering incentives and freebies to win new business, with the expectation you will recover the lost margin on future sales.

Upselling and cross-selling. Use the "this goes with that" mindset, and upsell and cross-sell on every transaction to your customers.

Products and flyers. Make up your own sales folder for everyday use.

Loss-leader products. Offer a loss-leader product, but only in conjunction with products that counterbalance the negative margin.

The product life cycle. Keep up with trends, read magazines, join Facebook and LinkedIn groups. Find the best source of information for the industry you work in.

A note on cold calling. Prepare and plan for your cold calls, pump yourself up with your favourite song, then go fishing and let me know the results (refer to step 10).

Retail therapy. Know your marketing material, ask lots of open-ended questions, then close the sale.

STEP 6: CLOSING THE SALE

Features and benefits

When closing the sale, it is important to reiterate the features and benefits of the product or products you have discussed in the sales call.

Features are what makes your product stand out from the crowd. They describe what it is and what makes it valuable, extraordinary or essential for the customer. Describing a *benefit* shows the customer what a particular feature can do for them, and tells them why they should buy the product.

It is important to fully understand the features and benefits of any product that you are selling, to sell it properly. Do all the research you can so that you have this covered.

Here are some examples of the features and benefits of some common products.

Umbrella. The latest umbrella features a wind-resistant frame and is made from stronger cloth called microweave fabric, which is rip-resistant.

The features here are the frame and the fabric.

The benefits are protection from the sun and rain, with the ability to withstand high winds without the umbrella collapsing or ripping.

Electric vehicle from Mitsubishi: the new Outlander PHEV

Here is the description from the Mitsubishi website:

The new Outlander PHEV (Plug-in Hybrid Electric Vehicle) is a ground-breaking vehicle that brings together the superior environmental performance and quietness of an electric vehicle (EV), the stability and handling of an AWD and the everyday practicalities and safety of an SUV. Sophisticated yet practical, the Outlander PHEV is the ultimate in intelligent motion and represents the next generation of hybrid and electric vehicles.[1]

In this above description, there seems to be a lot of features and no real benefits.

The features attract the potential customer into looking into the product in more detail, and in this case, the main benefits are:

- Lesser fuel consumption leads to some real cost savings.

- Lesser impact on the environment through reduced use of fossil fuels.

A good exercise is to get a sales brochure on a product; it doesn't really matter what it is. The brochure will go through all the features first, then finish off with the benefits.

Think about some products that you are interested in, and when you do your research, think about the features and benefits. You will soon see why these are so important to discuss in the sales process.

It is no good just handing a product to a customer without describing the features and benefits, as the customer may not always realise what they are.

As the salesperson, you are the expert, and knowledge is the key to getting a sale over the line, especially when the customer may then be promoting the product to their own customers.

The customer may even have enough trust in you to invite you to visit their customers to present your product. If you ever get asked to do this, it shows you have a strong relationship with your customer.

Better still, if you come back from such a presentation having made a sale for your customer, they will be very impressed, as you have helped them look professional and contributed to their bottom line.

Solution selling

When closing the sale, to get the maximum benefit we can offer the customer a solution, which will often get a better sales outcome.

People often buy things to fix a problem and, as a salesperson, our role is to offer a solution beyond what the customer expects.

If you refer back to the section "Research" in step 1, you will see I discussed how businesses diversify and move into new markets. To take advantage of this opportunity, as a salesperson, you need to put together all the pieces, just like a puzzle.

Let's use a simple role play in exploring solution selling. In this example, I'm a car salesman and you're the customer.

Your problem: Your car is using too much fuel and costing a fair penny to fill up.

You visit a car dealership and I'm not aware of your problem. I only know you don't just walk into a car dealership for no reason.

Me: Hello, how are you today?

You: Good, thanks.

Me: Can I help you with anything? Did something particular bring you in today?

You: Yes, my car is using quite a bit of fuel.

Me: That must be costing you a penny. I certainly have some vehicles here that will solve that issue. Can you tell me a bit more about what you will use your vehicle for? Do you have a family?

You: Day-to-day driving in the city, and yes, I will need an SUV, similar to my existing vehicle.

From there, the sales process would be to show the customer some vehicles, always starting with the most expensive and working back from there, and always discussing the features and benefits of each.

Always ask open-ended questions at the beginning. It's okay to ask two questions in a row; you want to get as much information as possible from the customer.

There is always a reason why a customer enters your store or outlet, and it is your job to find it out. In a different scenario, you may visit a customer at their workplace and they tell you their problem. The best thing you can do is take a lot of notes, then after you leave, review them to work out the best solution.

Hopefully, you come to a solution, but if you don't, you must let the customer know—don't leave them hanging.

In some cases, the solution may not be the product itself. For example:

- The goods may be organised to be supplied on a

pallet to specifically fit into a lift on a job site, making them easier to get to the required location.

- The goods are supplied in a box that can be used as a container for the small scraps from the job.

In both examples, the products may be similar to the competitors'; the difference is they offer a solution to a problem.

The above type of solution selling can be very successful, but you need to think outside the square to realise the opportunity.

Internal and external sales staff

When closing the sale, it is important that the customer understands that the communication and service will be the same when dealing with internal sales staff as when they deal with you.

As an external salesperson, what you say your business will do for your customer must actually happen when the customer goes into your branch to make a purchase or makes a phone call. Communication is the key with all staff.

Therefore, it is imperative that all internal sales staff understand the promotions and products you are show-ing, as well as the marketing strategies.

The only way they can understand is through education.

Before I go out to the market with any promotions, products or marketing strategies, I always brief internal sales staff so they understand them, should a customer ask about them.

A good example of a marketing and sales strategy I implemented for a customer explains the above principle in more detail.

I made a sales call on a customer with the plan to establish what our current share of his pie was. He had three suppliers, one that represented 40%, of his business, another that took 30%, and then we represented another 30%. With this information, I suggested to him that in the next month, if he could increase his percentage with us to 60%—meaning that our share would double—I would buy a voucher for his wife for a day spa.

He agreed he would try. I then sent an email to his admin email address, which his wife reads, explaining the arrangement. I also cc'd all the internal sales staff at the branch.

The next thing I heard from one of the internal sales staff was that he was speaking to the customer and his wife could be heard in the background telling him to buy everything from us. He achieved the target.

You are the leader of sales externally. It's a big responsibility. You must make sure that all the internal sales staff also get excited about promotions, new products and the like.

Make sure you share sales success stories with all the internal staff, and always share any positive feedback from external sales calls back to the relevant staff member. Get the team involved in any sales days or promotions; they need to have some buy-in and be a part of the results.

Negative feedback should also be shared, with the intended outcome being a solution to the issue, which you will often decide on as a group.

No sales equals no jobs!

Closing the sale

How do you know when to close the sale?

It is important to remember that closing a sale is not necessarily getting a physical order there and then. In most circumstances, it may, but it could also be getting an opportunity to offer a quote or to fill out an account form. It's taking away something you can act on so the communication between you and the customer keeps flowing.

Think of this example. A tradesman goes to a job and is asked to complete a particular task, generally to install or fix something. There is always an end point and something you can check to see if it works. This is where the tradesman gets his satisfaction.

For a salesperson, the satisfaction comes from getting a physical sale or a chance to take action on something.

A sales call can be compared to making a speech in a lot of ways. It has the same structure:

- the introduction;
- the body, which could be going through your prepared sales folder; and
- the conclusion, where you close the sale.

And there is only one way to close a sale, as described in the next section.

Always tell the truth in a sales call. Don't make stuff up, as I have seen others do. "What Goes Around Comes Around," to quote the title of a Justin Timberlake song, and you will eventually end up looking like a fool.

Never say no! No is a lost sale!

Ask for the order or opportunity

You are at the conclusion of your sales call. This is where a lot of salespeople fall down.

Not you, though. You will ask for the order or the chance to take action on something.

It's a simple process: quickly reflect on the key points of your call. Let's say, in this case, you have shown and discussed a new product. You've put that product in the customer's hand, told them the features and benefits and discussed the cost. Now, you just ask for the order.

In this case, the customer's name is Jon. Here's what you might say.

"Jon, now you've seen the product, held it and seen the opportunity it could create for your bottom line, please order a few so that you can have the opportunity to show your customers as well."

What's the worst that can happen? He can say no.

And it will happen at least some of the time, but if you refer back to step 3 and read over the rejection section, you will know how to handle the no.

At the end of the sales call, I always thank the customer for their business again and shake their hand. This is just a habit of mine, and it seems to work quite well.

Also make sure that you always have business cards in your wallet, and that you give the customer one before you leave.

After a sales call, I often quickly email or text myself anything that needs action, as a reminder so that I won't forget.

Make a sales system to suit your customer. Over the years, I have learned that sometimes all it takes to make a sale is to develop a sales system that is seamless for the customer. This will not be required for all customers, but there will be a small percentage that will need a specific sales system.

As an example, a builder I had been working with to get

their lighting and ceiling fan purchases simply wanted a $1,000 invoice from my company, as this is what they allowed for in the build cost to their customer. My company's system was based on inventory, and we had to develop a way to invoice the correct stock but give the builder a one-line $1,000 invoice. This involved a few people and many hours of thought and modification to our existing sales system, but resulted in extra sales in the long run.

Your current system may work for your business and the majority of your customers. However, if needed, spend as much time as it takes and work through different scenarios to create a sales system that suits your customer. You will find that the reward for this can be substantial relative to the effort involved.

Step 6 summary

Features and benefits. Make sure you research the features and benefits of the products you are selling before you make any sales calls.

Solution selling. Use open-ended questions to determine the customer's problem, then offer a solution to it with an array of products.

Internal and external sales staff. Keep internal sales staff informed about your efforts and results. Communicate with them regularly, verbally or via email.

Closing the sale. Your sales call is like a speech, with an introduction, body and conclusion. At the conclusion, you will aim to close the sale.

Ask for the order or opportunity. Just ask for the order or opportunity. Never forget this, as it is the most important action to take in this whole book. There is no point doing all the work, getting to this stage and failing to ask!

Now, get out there, make that physical sales call, and get the orders and opportunities. Your sales career depends on it!

STEP 7: FOLLOW-UP

Communication

Communication in business is extremely important—with customers, staff and suppliers. In some selling situations, we may feel we need to give a customer an answer immediately. But this is not always the case. It is important to give yourself time in some transactions, and the way to do this is to clarify with the customer how much time you have.

If the customer is in your showroom and you need time, divert them to having a look around and create some time that way. This will then let you gather the correct information by consulting supplier catalogues or websites. When the customer has finished looking around and comes back to you, the impression they get will be that you are professional and knowledgeable.

This perception can get you more sales and margin, as

you become the go-to person or the trusted advisor with various customers. Word of mouth also plays a big part in gaining referrals from customers.

Another example where time is important is promotions. Promotions will often state that they are only available while stocks last. Here, you would tell the customer that they should get their order in ASAP, as they could miss out on the promotional item, and that you will follow up with a phone call to confirm they have made their order within the timeframe.

Reporting

Most companies today will have a customer relationship management (CRM) system for their sales representatives. This technology has replaced paper call cards, which were often used to keep important information about the customer and kept somewhere like an expanding folder in the company car. The CRM is for all reporting on calls made on customers and is usually accessible on a tablet, smartphone or computer.

While we are talking about tablets and smartphones, I recently had what would have been a big issue, but luckily an honest person called me.

I was having lunch and working on my tablet down by the river, a lovely setting for lunch. I finished up and headed to my next call, which lasted about 30 minutes.

After that, I returned to my car and checked my mobile. I

always leave my mobile in my car or on silent, as I find it rude to answer and talk with someone else when you are at a customers' premises on their time. On my mobile, I noticed a call from a number that wasn't in my address book.

I called back and the gentleman asked me if I had been down by the river today. When I said yes, he told me I'd left my tablet on the table and that it was not locked, so he was able to check my email and get my number.

He left it with a couple staying just across from the table where I left it. I thanked him for being honest, but before I hung up, he suggested I put a code on the tablet and leave a business card in the cover.

All my devices now have password protection, and I have business cards in the covers of them all. I strongly suggest you do the same—and, of course, maybe don't leave your tablet out of your sight in the first place!

Some sales representatives see the CRM as a hindrance and entering data into it a pain in the backside. However, let me tell you that these systems have large benefits for both the company and the employee, and all businesses will be using them in the future.

Let's start with the employee. The CRM is an organisational tool, which helps you plan your weeks and months ahead, often with an option to create recurring call appointments so you don't have to keep scheduling them manually. Then, all you have to do is add comments on the call when you've completed it. It can be quite easy to input a list of all your customers and their call cycle for the year ahead, thus setting up your call plan.

A CRM can often also tell you when your customer is due for a call even if you haven't scheduled one. This keeps your customer contact flowing and ensures you don't forget anyone. The system will enable you to review notes from previous calls to the customer, which may have some follow-up jobs to be taken care of. You may even be able to see the notes of salespeople who served a particular customer before you, and if you ever move on to a different job, it will enable you to easily hand over your duties to the next person that comes along.

The CRM contains personal information on your customer, like their birthday and their favourite sporting team, so you can communicate with them more effectively. Financial information on your customer is also normally available, so you can get a quick snapshot of whether sales to them have gone up or down.

Now for the benefits to your company. The CRM is a great tool for management to review their sales representatives' activities and actions. In most cases, they can generate reports on such things as call rates and read information on calls entered by the sales representative.

Now, let me tell you a story about such a report.

As a committed and very well organised sales representative fairly early in my career, I religiously filled out all my call cards (there was no CRM in those days), and handed them to my manager every week for his review.

I spent a lot of time writing down the information I thought was relevant and, in some cases, needed action from management. It would only be fair to assume my call cards would be read and reviewed.

After a few months, it occurred to me that my manager and I had not discussed any of my call cards or any required actions. In fact, I started to wonder if he had read any of my call cards.

From this point and for the next few months, I would insert a call every week that was fake but should have stood out instantly if the cards were being read. The company I was working for required me, at that time, to call on electricians.

This is the exact call I entered in my call cards for the next few months:

Customer: Ghost Electrics

Call outcome: Casper seems very hard to track down. It's almost as though he doesn't exist. I have never seen him—or his van, as a matter of fact. Might need to engage Ghostbusters on this one.

When I approached my manager a few months later and asked him if he was reading and reviewing my call cards, he told me he was. It was quite a surprise that he had not contacted Ghostbusters and got them to catch up with Casper from Ghost Electrics.

He was very embarrassed and apologised profusely. From

that day forward, he paid attention to all his sales representatives' reports.

If you are a manager, it is only respectful that you read your sales representatives' reports. The sales representative put the time and effort in during their week to input the information, and for management to be on top of it can only help with sales, because then they and the sales representative will both understand the customer better.

The CRM is very beneficial if management intends on visiting a customer. They can quickly look up the customer's information, including the financials and the details of the last call a sales representative made on them. It helps to break the ice when you know a little about the customer before you call.

One of the biggest things in business is to follow up

Every sales call to a customer must result in something you can follow up on by taking action. It doesn't really matter what it is you have to follow up; what matters is that you keep the communication flowing between you and the customer.

This process of continually having something to follow up on every sales call to the customer will result either in a sale or development of your business relationship, which in turn will result in a sale.

Why would you go to all the trouble of preparing a quotation for a customer and then never follow it up?

You may as well not have done the physical sales call in the first place.

Most CRM systems have a way to make you follow up on anything that needs action. Some can link into your existing sales system and import the information into the CRM. Whatever system or means of reporting the business you work for has in place, make sure that if your business does a quotation for a customer, that it gets followed up. The customer asked for the quote for a reason.

Always allow time in your week to review your CRM and make sure your calls are on track. This amazing tool has made many disorganised people into the most organised sales representatives in many companies, resulting in increases in both sales and margin.

A note on cold calling

The most important thing when doing a cold call is to make sure that some sort of follow-up is required on completion of the call. This initial follow-up will form the basis of your business relationship with the potential customer, and you must give that action priority.

If a customer says they will email or call you after your sales call, don't wait for it to happen. If you have not heard from the customer after a few days, follow it up.

With most cold calls, my follow-up would be to pick up

the completed account form or to tell the customer their account is open and get the first sale.

Retail therapy: Follow-up

If giving a retail customer a catalogue or another type of product reference, ensure you put a sticker with your business details on it. This way, they will remember where to go when they need the product.

I always kept a stapler and business cards in my vehicle so I could attach my business card to the brochure I left with the customer. Always get the name, number and email of the person if possible. This is so you can ring or email them about any new product information or specials in future.

As discussed under "Communication" above, allow yourself time to do whatever you need to—be it organising your information or researching a solution. When I needed to clarify a time frame with a customer, I tended to extend it to allow for any hiccups. However, in most circumstances, the time frame was more than generous enough, and the customer was very satisfied when I called earlier than expected.

In the same breath, if you find out that you cannot meet the time frame for some reason, a follow-up call to communicate this to the customer is crucial. Make sure you get their correct details at the time of the transaction so you can call them if need be.

Another great follow-up tool is to offer your retail customers a discount card they can hand to family and friends. This will promote word of mouth, which is the best free advertising any business can get.

Email etiquette

A few years back, the company I worked for was having a promotion and the sales manager at the time wanted to email the information out to all the customers.

Our CRM had all the email addresses of the customers from all the various sales representatives in their particular territories.

The sales manager handed the email job to his administrative assistant, who then collated all the email addresses and sent out the promotional information.

Later that day, a customer called who seemed a bit abrupt and asked for the administrative assistant. He said she had shared his personal information with his competitors, and that he owned his email address and it was up to him who he wished to share it with. All the email addresses of the customers were in the to field. Always email to your own email address and bcc to everyone else if you are doing a group email.

If you are going on holidays, ensure that you not only change the voicemail message on your smartphone but also set up an auto-reply on your email. This is for two reasons.

First, you are on holidays and the last thing you want to be doing is responding to emails and phone calls. Your wife or partner won't be happy!

Second, if you don't do this, your customers will expect the same level of customer service or response time as when you are at work, which can be hard to achieve on holidays.

Make sure you leave an alternative contact phone number and email address on your voicemail message and email auto-reply, and let the person whose details you are giving know about the situation and the level and speed of customer service you expect.

A couple of other things to consider on the subject of emails:

- Always check over your email before you send it. Make sure the to, cc and bcc fields all contain the right contacts, make sure the content is correct, and make sure the attachment, if any, is what it is meant to be. Doing the above can save you a lot of embarrassment.
- When you get an email from somebody, always reply with a simple thanks, as this will acknowledge to the sender that you have received the message.

Events and functions

Having organised and successfully run many events and functions during my career, I can tell you that follow-up is extremely important if you want to get great numbers to your event.

Here is the normal procedure I follow for an event:

1. Have marketing make a flyer representing the event and subject matter, with a contact to respond to and an RSVP date.
2. Send out a group email, normally three weeks out from the event or function, with all contacts bcc'd, quickly introducing the event and attaching the flyer.
3. A week out from the event, personally call each contact. If there are many, get the help of another sales representative or staff member. This process is vitally important, as this is where you will get a fair idea of the numbers that are going to attend.
4. On the day of the event or the evening before, send out a group text to all customers that have said they are attending, telling them not to forget, and giving them the event details again. Also ask them to text or call if they aren't going to make it.

By putting the time and effort into following the above

four steps, I've had great numbers attending all the events and functions I've been involved in over the years.

Step 7 summary

Communication. Give yourself time in your sales transactions.

Reporting. Always do your reporting by keeping your CRM up to date; it's a sales tool.

A note on cold calling. You must plan for some follow-up; it's non-negotiable.

Retail therapy. Get all the customer's details if you don't make the sale there and then.

Email etiquette. Never send a group email out by putting all the names in the to field. Always send the email to yourself as the main contact and bcc the group.

Events and functions. Follow the four steps I recommend to achieve maximum attendance. Make a flyer, send a group email three weeks out, call each contact a week before the event and text a reminder on the day or the night before.

STEP 8: DEVELOPING
RELATIONSHIPS

Relationships

The key to all business is relationships, be they with customers, suppliers, staff or management.

Just like a marriage, business relationships will have their ups and downs, and how you handle them is the most important thing. Communication is the key to all successful relationships, so if you keep the communication channels open, your business relationship will have every chance of being strong and prosperous.

The most common way to tell if your relationship is becoming stronger is when the customer gives you a nickname. For me personally, when a customer called me "Matty", I knew I had a good relationship with them. That entitled me to call the customer by their nickname, too.

If you have followed steps 1 through 7 correctly, you will

have started a great foundation for a business relationship, but it doesn't end there. Business relationships are long-term, and in most cases will last for many years to come.

The greatest thing about forming a business relationship and strengthening it over the years is that it will eventually let you ask for a greater share of the customer's business. In some cases, that greater share will just come to you naturally.

When selling, you must respect your customer's customers. Never bypass your customer to get to theirs; always get their approval first.

For example, if you wanted to get a share of a builder's business—let's say the light fixtures they buy—and your core customer is an electrician that does work for that builder, you would talk to your core customer (the electrician) before going to the builder.

The reason is that there is already a strong relationship between the builder and electrician. This should be used to your advantage; don't go against it.

The customer will also usually share information with you about your competitors. For example, they will still receive information from competitors, who will still be chasing the customer's business. Because of your relationship, a customer may share your competitors' information with you freely. This gives you an advantage from knowing what your competitors are doing in the market.

I recently got a text message from one of my good customers, with a photo attached of my competitor's specials at the time. This enabled me to react and get some orders from other customers before the competitor did.

It also showed me that the relationship I had with my customer meant he would prefer to get the goods from me rather than my competition—though I would, of course, have to match the special pricing.

My experience is that over time, your customers can become great personal friends. Although this can be very satisfying to achieve, you still need to keep friendship and business separate.

From the personal perspective, you should know your customer's birth date, their favourite sporting team, and their spouse and children's names.

If you are working in a service type of industry, a way to grow your relationship is to always ring your customer before you call in, and offer to bring anything they may need with you.

While I was working as a sales representative in the automotive electrical industry, I would load up my company car with all the common components purchased by auto electricians before I headed off on my road trips out of town. I would also send all my customers a text message the day before to remind them I was coming.

In the beginning, I got sales for the common components

I kept in my vehicle, and continued to do so, but then the customers changed their habits.

When they got my text message to say I was coming, they would send me orders or ring the store for other parts as well as the common items, since they knew I was coming through town the next day. The sales from these out-of-town customers started to grow as we got a greater share of their business due to our service.

Our margin also grew because the common components, some of which were loss-leaders, were complemented by other parts that made up for the low margin on the common ones.

It is also a great idea to occasionally arrange a lunch or coffee meeting outside of both your workplaces. During a lunch meeting, there will be fewer distractions, and the customer will feel more relaxed and comfortable. You will both listen more, and the customer will answer open-ended questions with more thought, giving you more information to work with.

Offer your customer a fair and reasonable price along with great service and quick handling of complaints, and your relationship will become very strong—so strong that, in some cases, achieving as much as a 90–100% share of their purchases will become a realistic target.

Creating a call plan

One of the most important things you can do is to ensure you clarify how often the customer would like you to visit them. There is nothing worse than being a pain in the butt to a customer by over-servicing them.

You must also remember that if you always create an action from every call to them, you will always have a plan for when to contact them next, even though this may be a verbal rather than physical call. Today, it's common to email regularly about specials and new products, and this is also a great communication channel.

You must always have something of value to show the customer; you need to make sure they see you as worthwhile and as someone who is helping their business.

Another great initiative can be to organise some calls to customers and take along senior people in the business you work for. Doing this makes the customer feel important and puts your company at the top of their mind. It also enables management to get a better understanding of their customers' needs.

It is very important that if you are travelling with someone else in your vehicle, and you choose to answer a phone call thorough hands-free, the first thing you do is tell the caller you are not alone. I remember one time when a colleague of mine had his children in the car and did not tell me when I called him. Some of the language I used was inappropriate for a child to hear, and when he did inform me, I was quite embarrassed.

Make this a habit whenever someone else is in your vehicle, and you will save yourself some embarrassment.

Some customers may suggest they do not need to see you, which is fine, but as discussed previously, you can still make a phone call to thank them for their business, and this goes a long way. You should do this quarterly, and can schedule it in your call plan. You would also obviously still target these customers with email specials and new product information.

In the early days before CRM, I developed a call plan folder that contained all my customers, who I organised into groups, e.g., Geelong 1, Geelong 2, Torquay 1, Torquay 2 and Apollo Bay.

Under each of these groups, there would be around eight customers, and the call plan folder contained any relevant notes on them. Grouping customers this way then enabled me to enter them into the CRM when my company introduced it some time later.

After spending time in January of each year inputting all my groups into the CRM and making the call appointments recur as required, I would have my annual plan as a guide and starting point for the next 12 months.

Want to learn more about call planning?
I've developed a training video at
knackofselling.com.au/members.

Join today and take a look at this video and others.

Social functions

Organise some social functions with your customers. This will require some after-hours work, but the results for that effort will be nothing short of outstanding.

Generally, when your management sees you going the extra mile, they will be more lenient when you ask for some time off down the track.

It is always important to make sure you offer two types of social function: one for business owners and staff, and one for the families of the owners and the staff, if this is feasible and within your budget.

Both types of social function involve the same principles of relationship-building, but the second type lets you add a more personal touch to your future sales calls, as you will now know all the families associated with the business.

A customer recently asked me if I could source some football tickets for him. When my manager contacted our head office to help with this, we were able to get the customer and his family some really good tickets. This allowed me to follow up with him the following week, and I was not afraid to ask for an order, as I knew he appreciated what we had done for him and his family. In fact, he emailed senior management and thanked them for the chance to take his family to the football, and told them how great a time they all had.

Although I wasn't physically there, the customer and his family will no doubt remember the experience and associate the memory with the company I represent. This creates a talking point for future sales calls, as we can discuss football to bring back his happy memories.

If you can incorporate some education and training into your social functions, it can go a long way towards you being seen as a trusted advisor and a person who is trying to help your customers' businesses. Just make sure you get it done before the beer and wine comes out!

You may wish to involve other local businesses in your social function, which are involved in the industry you work in or who can help your customers in some way. For example, at one function I organised, I invited an accountant, an osteopath and a WorkSafe representative to come and talk to a group of electricians. The accountant could help with the electricians' books and tax, the osteopath with their sore backs from climbing up ladders and being in confined spaces, and the WorkSafe representative discussed the responsibilities of an electrician to provide a safe workplace for their staff.

Although this social function had no direct link to selling anything, what it did was position myself and the company I worked with as being genuinely interested in the well-being of our customers.

Always keep up with current news and sport, as you can

always use this knowledge as an icebreaker, especially if you know the latest on the team your customer barracks for.

The aim of social functions is to get to the forefront of your customer's mind, so that when they go to buy their goods or supplies, you are the first person they think of.

When organising social functions, make sure you create a great flyer with all the necessary details, or have marketing create one, and email it to all the relevant customers. Send it to all other parties involved (e.g., suppliers) too, to show your professionalism and give them an overview of the function.

Prepare a schedule of events with your flyer, so you can let participants know what will be happening and when. But don't send this to your customers, unless you want them only showing up to the parts they think are relevant to themselves.

Text reminders to all customers the day before, or on the day of the event, to maximise attendance

Also keep an event registration database, and after the function, use it to make sure customers' details in your CRM are up to date.

Losing a customer

In business, there is always the chance of losing a customer for various reasons, some in your control, others not.

Here are a few examples of situations I've experienced over the years.

Unfortunately, we cannot live forever. Customers grow old and retire, and some may die unexpectedly. This is out of your control. What is in your control is to recognise when this happens with your customer base, and actively chase new, younger customers to replace the older, retiring customers and the unlucky ones who have passed away.

One of my business's internal staff was once updating customer details and contacted a customer's wife only to find the customer had passed away. This was very embarrassing for her. If you find out a customer has died, inform your senior management and ensure that the CRM is updated to reflect this unfortunate part of life.

Some customers may get so upset at the forgetfulness involved in calling for someone who has passed away that they decide to change suppliers.

In another instance, I caused a customer to change suppliers by starting to charge the customer freight.

I was more concerned about the freight than the customer, not realising that the margin on his account more than covered the small freight charges involved in getting the goods to him. The customer was upset as he had never been charged freight before; my competitors had never charged him freight either.

I made a mistake, but I learned from it. This is very important, so you can make sure it doesn't happen again.

Sales days and specials

Sales days and specials are often aimed at new customers or those that don't yet deal with the business you represent.

It is very important that you offer all your sales days and regular specials to all your customers. You don't want a great customer to get offended because they weren't offered the same special as a customer that does not yet deal with your business.

When having a ring-around sales day, you will come across a few scenarios.

First, the customer may not answer, and you will leave a message.

Second, you may talk to the customer, but they don't have the time to review your offer, and ask that you email them the information.

Third, you may get an order and thank the customer.

All these scenarios require follow-up via a phone call, either to follow up the message you left or the email you sent, or to tell the customer when to expect delivery of their order. Be sure to make the follow-up call, as this is often when you will get an order. In the third scenario, it gives you the chance to provide great customer service by communicating with the customer about their order, bolstering your position with them.

Always make sure you have the stock available to satisfy all specials orders. If not, make sure you inform the customer of the timeline for delivery. Make sure a member of staff rings customers when their goods arrive from your supplier. This shows you have kept them in mind and know they are waiting for their order.

Rewards cards

Today, there are many offers in the rewards-card space that aim to attract customers, offering a perk of some kind if they continually buy goods from one supplier or brand.

These programs can be very beneficial to the sales effort, and it is worth working out the best offer to suit your particular business.

Generally, most of these programs are based on sales, and are targeted to all customers, with the cost of the reward built into the margin on the products involved.

One of the latest rewards campaigns that I've participated in is the Woolworths Rewards card. I keep this card in my wallet and use it every time I visit a Woolworths supermarket. Eventually, I earn ten dollars after several months.

I have never calculated how much I have to spend to get the ten dollars, but it must be a fair bit, as it doesn't happen very often. Mind you, I share my business between Aldi and Woolworths.

The benefit to Woolworths from this rewards system is that they start to gather valuable information about what their customers buy, and then use this in their marketing to entice you back, or to encourage you to buy further items if you shop online. The emails I now receive from Woolworths specifically offer specials on products I have bought recently or regularly.

If you can offer a rewards system as a part of your selling process, there is no doubt you will benefit from sales and margin growth. It's developing the right system that is the hard part; it's often through trial and error that the best system is achieved.

Become the trusted advisor

If you earn the title *trusted advisor*, it means you have business acumen. It means you have the experience, training, knowledge and subject-matter expertise to be trusted to advise your clients well. It also indicates a certain set of behaviours.

When you get to the stage in the selling process where you become the customer's trusted advisor, you know you have made it.

This is the ultimate in relationship development: the customer sees you as someone they can trust and get involved with their business. They will ask you a number of things, which sometimes may have nothing to do with your business, because they see you as having a wealth of knowledge on multiple subjects.

If you are in regular daily contact with a customer, the sales and margin with them can grow exponentially, and they may begin to take up a fair chunk of your time. You are their number one contact in your industry—the go-to person. You've gotten to this stage through hard work, by applying the ten steps from *The Knack of Selling* to your daily operations.

If you can achieve this with all your customers, you will be very successful, but it is near-impossible to maintain, as you never get more time. There are only 24 hours in a day, after all!

By becoming the trusted advisor, you have ticked all the boxes and are then helping the business to grow and develop.

This is where step 9, which deals with customer and staff lifecycles, becomes very important. If you do not follow step 9, you will not be able to cope with the demand you have created, and both you and your customers will start to fall away from the business.

This also means that the business may need to employ more staff. If you look back to the beginning of the book under the heading "Is Selling an Art?", you will see me talking about satisfaction.

Retail therapy: Developing relationships

In the retail environment, relationship development can happen in a number of ways.

First, as discussed previously in this step, rewards cards can entice repeat business from your clients in the retail environment. They also enable counter sales staff to recognise customers by name when they scan their rewards cards, making transactions a bit more personal.

Second, staff who are the first point of call can create happy feelings within the customer by being welcoming and positive, and this alone can put the business first in the customer's mind when they next think about a product it offers.

Third, a great website is crucial to relationship development today. If your business offers a well-presented and easy-to-use website, your customers will keep coming back. Many websites even now offer a live chat option, which is a great communication channel that can be used to close a sale.

Step 8 summary

Relationships. The key to business, relationships enable you to get a greater share of your customers' business.

Creating a call plan. Establish and maintain a call plan to stay in contact as frequently as the customer tells you they would like.

Social functions. Functions are a chance to develop relationships with customers and their staff and family members outside of the daily business environment.

Losing a customer. It will happen, and it's important to recognise the reasons why.

Sales days and specials. Offer any sales days and specials to all your customers, not just those that haven't yet done business with you.

Rewards cards. Rewards cards and programs can be a great way to develop relationships with your customers.

Become the trusted advisor. This is the ultimate relationship position to be in, but be careful and ensure you move on to step 9.

Retail therapy. Great staff and a great website are key to building relationships.

STEP 9: OUT WITH THE OLD, IN WITH THE NEW

It seems a bit harsh if we say we want to move out old staff and customers, but it's all part of doing business, and often it happens naturally.

The customer lifecycle

As discussed in step 5, products have lifecycles. So do customers. Ensuring that you are on top of your customer lifecycles is crucial if your business is to continue to grow.

You should categorise your customers every quarter to ensure you understand where they all sit in the customer lifecycle graph, which is made up of four phases.

Phase 1—New in business: 1–5 years

These customers are very important to have, as they are the future of your business. They do come with a little more risk, as some will succeed and some will not, but you must ensure you have a good percentage in this category.

Phase 2—Growing in business: 5–10 years

These have become good customers over the first five years of their business's operation. They have good business sense and ethics. Work hard to keep these customers, as after having survived five years, they are likely to continue in business for many years to come.

Phase 3—Mature in business: 10–20 years

These customers are well established, and the core of your business. They value your business and all that you offer. You still need to work hard to keep these customers, though, as customers in this phase are low-risk, which often makes them the first targets of competitors.

Phase 4—Retiring from business: 20+ years

In this phase, the customer is nearing the end of the customer lifecycle. Normally, three things can happen in this phase.

One. For a family business, a new generation can take over and continue to grow it into the future.

Two. The owners sell the business, and a new owner takes it on and puts in a lot of time and money to keep it growing into the future.

Three. The owners retire and the business retires with them.

Here is an example of a good customer profile to have in your business.

XYZ Business has 100 customers, which fall into the following categories:

- 32 customers in business 1–5 years (phase 1)
- 33 customers in business 5–10 years (phase 2)
- 28 customers in business 10–20 years (phase 3)
- 7 customers in business 20+ years (phase 4)

Here is an example of a poor customer profile not to have in your business.

ZYX Business has 100 customers, which fall into the following categories:

- 3 customers in business 1–5 years (phase 1)
- 7 customers in business 5–10 years (phase 2)
- 35 customers in business 10–20 years (phase 3)
- 55 customers in business 20+ years (phase 4)

Your customer profile will continually change over time as customers move through their lifecycle. You and your sales management should be well across this and review it consistently.

Make the shift

Over time, as your business develops and your relationships get stronger, you will find it impossible to maintain the customer-service level that you achieved at the beginning.

This is where your internal sales staff become crucial in allowing you to keep chasing new business while offering the same service levels as you did at the start. It may also be that your business will need new employees as it grows.

I mentioned earlier in the book that a sales representative is very satisfied when their business grows to a point where it needs more staff. It is the ultimate point for a business to get to.

To make the shift happen, the first thing you need to do is communicate it to your customer. You need to be open and honest in your conversations.

I know what you are thinking: what is *the shift*?

It's all to do with staff and customers, and putting the pieces of the puzzle together.

We need to shift *staff* into the positions that maximise their productivity and best use their skills while keeping them happy and challenged.

We need to shift *customers* into transacting with the right staff in the right positions, who fit their personality and can meet their needs and wants. These staff members will handle most transactions and complaints from customers.

This process allows sales representatives to move on, chase

more new business, and look for new markets and opportunities.

Here are some examples from my career.

Example 1

"The time has come to develop our younger staff further. For this to happen, they need to be given opportunities. As you are a loyal and understanding customer, we are giving you the opportunity to embrace this change."

After introducing a customer to an impending shift in your business like this, clarify that they are happy with the change and reassure them that you will still be calling in with a younger representative at least every quarter.

Where businesses I have worked for have handed accounts over to younger staff professionally, and with good communication, we have had no issues. As a senior sales representative, it doesn't take much to call a customer to check everything is as you left it, and that they are still happy with the arrangement.

You can also monitor sales from the customer. A decline should raise questions about whether the customer is really happy. An increase may prompt you to ask—was the senior sales representative doing a good job in the first place?

Example 2

I have had meetings with internal sales staff and asked them to start communicating with customers more often than they normally would. Soon after, they became the account manager for the account. All specials, back orders and account queries now became the responsibility of those internal sales staff.

Staff start to organise visits to the customer and over time, without any hiccups whatsoever, the customer just gets used to the new employee calling on them, or they become happy to phone the branch or call in and see the internal sales staff member.

If a customer asks why the person they are dealing with has changed, you can give the simple answer that the old sales representative has moved on to developing new markets, and will be in touch with an opportunity shortly to help the customer develop their business further.

Customers: The good, the bad, and the ugly

Let's talk about customer positioning.

The good customer

- is honest
- has a good personality
- is happy
- pays bills within terms
- is someone we are happy to take as many sales from as possible

These customers need to be held on to for as long as possible and given the maximum amount of service possible. They respect your business and what you offer, but you must not get complacent.

The bad customer

- has a bad attitude
- is more demanding than a normal customer
- has cash-flow issues
- is someone whose business we are happy to take a percentage of with a good margin

These customers keep you on your toes and demand more than the good customer, but don't respect your business and what you offer. Put simply, they are a player, and may be quite arrogant at times. Your business will take whatever it can get, but at a margin to compensate for the demand and attitude.

The ugly customer

- makes no payment for more than double the length of the terms for the account
- is hard to contact and never returns calls
- only calls when the competitor does not have the product
- is someone we would prefer not to do business with, or only for an extreme margin

Let the competitors have these customers. If you do have to transact with a customer like this, make sure you make some extreme margin, as you won't get paid for a while.

Ultimately, a business should have 80% good customers and 20% bad customers, with a goal to replace the bad customers with good customers won from competitors over time.

Step 9 summary

The customer lifecycle. Monitor customers' position in their lifecycle regularly to make sure you have a good customer profile.

Make the shift. Put the pieces of the puzzle together with staff and customers. Introduce your customers to new staff so that your senior salespeople can continue to pursue new business.

Customers: The good, the bad, and the ugly. Aim to have 80% good customers in your business.

STEP 10: THE SELLING IS DONE.
CELEBRATE AND WORK ON YOU.

Celebrate your sales results and success

It is very important that you celebrate your sales results and success with your team, and explain how you got the results.

Often, when success is discussed, more success results.

The company I work for recently had a promotion where a customer would receive a jacket if they ordered a certain amount and used the business's online platform.

This promotion had a number of hurdles to get through for the customer to receive their jacket. When I discussed this with the branch manager, we decided we needed to make the process as seamless as possible while also educating customers about our online offer.

We set about to register as many customers as possible to our online platform, a simple process that took around two minutes of the customers' time. Then we offered them a special on the products that had to be bought in the promotion, and also let them build their order to the required value.

This was seamless for the customer; they got special pricing and a jacket all in the one deal. They also now had the facility to access the online platform, and that created the chance for a follow-up call from our team to explain the full offer of the online platform at a later date.

In the background, there were a number of steps required for the team to process the orders, and together we got the job done and were one of the top-performing teams in the business for this particular promotion.

Sharing in success like this creates a fantastic positive culture within a team environment, and this comes across when dealing with customers.

In monthly team meetings, we would always go around the room and share our success stories. This was a great opportunity for all staff to contribute and tell their stories to the rest of the team.

A word on time management

Time management is critically important in sales.

A few things I've discussed earlier in this book relate directly to time management and should be kept in mind. Hence, I will repeat them below.

There are approximately 172 days each year available for face-to-face selling. Therefore, time management is crucial to make the most of these days.

By organising your calls into groups and then entering them into your CRM for the year ahead, you will have a plan for the 172 available sales days.

Today, many time-management apps are available, all similar but subtly different. Simply Google "time-management apps" and you will find many options. Most have free trials, so try a few and see if they suit your particular needs.

Rather than holding all meetings in one particular location, you can now have meetings with your counterparts no matter where they are.

A great product for online meetings is Zoom. You can simply download the Zoom app and you are away. This technology saves time and is very efficient, giving you crystal-clear video of the person you are talking with, and the ability to review files from the meeting host. Give it a try for your next meeting.

Emails are a great communication channel, but it is easy to get bogged down in them. Many emails are not directed to you and therefore don't need a response.

You should allocate time in your day to review and take action on emails. Generally, the best time is first thing in the morning. During this time, you can review all emails and determine which ones need action that day. Address all those first and then the less important ones.

Make this a habit—allocate a period in the day to review emails and avoid checking email outside of that time. You will find it helps to manage your time during the day. If something is very important, most people will call you first before they email you.

A good way to get a message to your customers is to have a training or information session on a particular topic. You can then get multiple customers together at once and kill a few birds with one stone!

When offering specials and sales, put your customers in a contact group and send out a group text or email with the relevant information—but make sure recipients' numbers and email addresses are not shown to others. Address the email to yourself and put all other recipients in the bcc field.

I spend a fair bit of time driving, and in preparation before I hit the road, I would put together a list of actions I could take while driving. Most of the time, I would have a list of quotes that we had put out and would call customers to chase them up.

You will need to screen mobile-phone calls. I personally would not answer any calls from a private number, letting them go to voicemail and returning the call if the caller left a message.

I would limit any personal calls during the day, inbound or out, making or returning them during a lunch break.

After a meeting, I would review any phone calls I had missed and then decide on an action matching their importance. If I were visiting multiple clients in an area, I would wait to call people back while I was driving to another destination, as this would save time I might otherwise be sitting around calling people back. It would also make the trip feel faster.

It is also important to recognise that there is a time limit when calling on a customer, and it is the customer who determines this. You need to read the customer and ensure you are not overextending your stay.

Be a hunter and a farmer

There are sales representatives, and then there are hunters!

You need to be a hunter. And just like a hunter in the bush, you will seek out your prey and then go in for the kill—armed not with a gun, of course, but with an attitude of "never give up" and "seek and you shall find".

Here are a couple of examples of being a hunter.

Imagine you have planned your call and are at the physical sales call. While there, you look around and hunt for opportunities. You find some products that are from your competitors and make a mental note of them. While achieving your planned objectives, you've also created an opportunity to offer an alternative to your competitor's products at a future sales call.

The way I would handle this is to take a sample of your alternative product on your next call to start the conversation. Get the customer to commit to trying the product you offer, then ask for the order and slowly repeat this process over time to get more of their product portfolio.

Another way to hunt is to research your competitors and their customers. If your competitor doesn't know you, visit their store as a random shopper. See what they are offering and how their customer service rates. Park nearby and watch what customers are visiting; you may see some opportunities for new cold calls on customers you were not aware of.

Just like in real hunting, sometimes you will get a kill and sometimes you won't, but you must be a hunter to have the chance. So be a hunter and hunt out the opportunities.

You also need to think outside the square to keep your customers interested in your business. Offer them promotions, training, rewards and nights out for dinner. Keep your business at the forefront of their minds.

Know yourself

self-knowledge   noun [mass noun]

Understanding of oneself or one's own motives or character.

— Oxford Dictionary of English

Self-knowledge is often gained over time. You discover your strengths and weaknesses, learn how your mind works and how to control your emotions and feelings. You know your body and what it can handle.

Self-knowledge = happiness.

Sometimes self-discovery comes when you are at your lowest point (we all get there at some stage). Reflect and work out how to get back to a higher point.

I know one of my weaknesses is that I tend to butt in during conversation. It can be really annoying to the other person, I'm told. It's something I'm aware of and continually try to get better at each day. It's a case of listening and holding back until the other person pauses; then that's the opportunity to add your two bob's worth.

If that's all he has to worry about, you may say, then he's got it good!

Let me tell you that I went through a lot of pain and

problems to get to this point of self-understanding, but that's another book.

There are also professional people who can help you on your path to self-discovery: doctors, psychologists, community groups and specialist counselling can all help you.

When I was at my lowest points in life, I sought help via a community group of people who all had the same issue. This helped me tremendously as a person. I visited a specialist counsellor and, once again, it helped me tremendously.

There are always people who will listen and help when you are at your lowest point; seek them out and use them.

There are many personal development books available to read; these will give you a better understanding of how to gain self-knowledge.

It takes a long time and a lot of effort before you can understand yourself fully. I truly believe it's a life-long journey. Once you start on the road to self-discovery, you will never leave it, and you will likely never want to.

Sales conferences

No doubt as you become successful in sales, you will get an opportunity to attend many sales conferences with your colleagues, as I have over the years with the various companies I have worked for.

I have been lucky enough to not only attend many in Australia, but also in Austria, South Africa, Penang in Malaysia, Hong Kong and, most recently, Koh Samui in Thailand.

There is one conference experience I will never forget.

Very early in my career, as a new young sales representative with a new company, I was eager to impress my fellow senior colleagues who, unknown to me, had a lot of conference experience behind them.

The lesson from this experience was, "Play hard, but always make sure you are on time and ready to go the next morning." This is the most important message you will receive about conferences, so make sure if you play hard (i.e., have a few drinks) you are still up and ready the next morning. Set your alarm, ring reception for a wake-up call, or even ask staff to come to your room and get you up. *Do whatever you must to get up and be on time the next morning!*

Most of my fellow salespeople who have not achieved this are no longer in a sales job.

There was only one thing that saved me: the national sales manager.

After having a few—and a few more—I did not set my alarm, so I did not wake up on time the next morning. I woke up late and, in fact, had turned my mobile phone off. The first message I got when I turned it back on was from my boss, who was not happy and basically said I was an embarrassment to him and my fellow employees. I felt sick!

Then I had someone knock on my door, and it was not reception. It was a colleague who was happy to see me on my opening the door, but gave me the bad news that there were 50 people in a conference room, and I was going to have to make an entrance in front of them all, knowing I was in a lot of trouble.

This was one of the worst feelings I have ever had, especially as that morning the company had paid a professional speaker to talk to the group, which would have cost quite a few dollars. It was a very, very long day, and I have not forgotten it.

After the day ended, we once again had dinner and drinks with the senior staff of the company. I had water!

What happened next is one of the best lessons for conferences I have ever learned, and has saved many from the embarrassment I experienced.

The general manager came up to me and explained, to my astonishment, that he was not that upset with me, as he understood I was young and had made a mistake, as long as I had learned from it.

He was, however, very upset with his national sales manager, who was sharing a room with me but failed to check on me before he left in the morning.

Everyone was worried about me, my whereabouts and my safety. Had something bad happened to me?

As in *Top Gun*, always look out for your wingman! If you haven't seen this movie, get on Netflix and watch it now: it's a classic.

From this day forward, I have always made sure that whoever I have been rooming with, we make sure we don't leave the room in the morning without the other person being awake and ready to go. It's a handshake agreement.

By implementing this, I have saved many from embarrassment and educated a few along the way.

As a rule, you should be able to have a great time and enjoy yourself; never step over that line. If you don't know the line I'm talking about, one day you will understand, as we all make mistakes. When you cross it, you will feel terrible physically (maybe with some sore stomach muscles) and worse mentally, knowing you are in a lot of trouble!

Presentations

As a salesperson, it is imperative that you master the skill of talking in front of people, especially your peers.

At school, I was always fearful of getting up in front of the class and talking. Through continued training and practising throughout my career, I mastered the skill of presenting and now can confidently speak in front of any audience.

As a salesperson, you never know when your presenting skills will be needed.

Recently, a colleague and I called on a TAFE college to discuss our business and also show some new products. The teachers were very impressed with the product I showed them, and immediately asked me to present in front of some 30 students.

These students knew nothing of the business I represented, so I had to explain the business and its history in detail. After that, we discussed the new product and I handed some samples to the students to use.

Afterwards, the teachers were very appreciative of my presentation, and I gave it to a total of three classes that morning. This helped me build my relationship with the key contact at the TAFE.

It's all about confidence and knowledge of the subject you are presenting. If you have the knowledge, you should have no issue; it's when you don't know your stuff that you can come undone.

Another great thing to try is Toastmasters. This is an organisation of people who gather to develop their skills in public speaking.

By attending Toastmasters sessions, you will develop the confidence to speak freely in front of customers and peers. Visit the Toastmasters site at www.toastmasters. org.au to find out more.

Another thing to consider when presenting is to make

sure that you get all the details of who attends. This is as simple as having a sheet of paper and asking the attendees for their full name, the business they represent, and their mobile number and email address.

This will give you the chance to follow up with attendees to gather feedback, and also to chase up potential sales of whatever you are presenting about.

Mental health and exercise

Sales is a mentally challenging job; you always need to be thinking on your feet.

Your mind will always be very busy, pressure can mount if sales are declining, and new selling techniques will need to be created and implemented. New marketing strategies need to be developed and tested, and the list goes on.

When sales are increasing, you are still thinking about how to maintain sales, how to be different from your competitors and how to keep your business's edge.

All this work for your mind will eventually catch up with you if you don't have an outlet.

I have seen many salespeople over my career, including myself, continually working after hours to make sure that they are on top of the game. They spend time researching new trends, new products from suppliers, and competitors' websites, always in their own time, when their focus should be on other interests or family.

You need to be full of knowledge to excel in sales, and

you need to have followed all the ten steps in *The Knack of Selling*. All this work takes time, and there is generally no time to work on improving your skills during normal business hours. This is why investment from companies in training outside of the normal working environment can be so effective in developing key sales staff.

The remedy for all this mental exertion during and after business hours is to wind down with some exercise. You must fit a minimum of 30 minutes of exercise into your schedule each day.

Get yourself a fitness watch and make sure you are getting these 30 minutes of exercise in. This is the key to being a sales rep who excels.

Even during your lunch break, you can find a local park with a path (just Google "local path") and spend 30 minutes walking, taking in the environment and fresh air around you. Not only will you get your exercise in, but the fresh air will relax your mind, and you will feel reinvigorated when you get back to selling.

Put a reminder to take those 30 minutes in your CRM if you have to. Tell your boss your goal—I'm sure they will be impressed. Make this non-negotiable; get it done every day.

Exercise makes the endorphins flow in your brain, and will prepare your mind for the next day or week of selling.

You must also watch your food and alcohol intake, as this

affects your mental health. A lot of sales representatives are overweight; it can come with the job, but this is not necessarily true. You choose what you eat and how much you drink.

I personally attend my local Parkrun event every week. This is a community run hosted by local volunteers on a 5km timed course along a beautiful river.

In the beginning, it was very difficult, as I was not used to running, but after a few runs, my body realigned and it became easier, as I was obviously getting fitter.

Parkrun is held on a Saturday morning, so it's a great way to finish the working week and start the weekend. Afterwards, you feel refreshed and your mind is clear.

Visit **www.parkrun.com.au**. to find your local Parkrun event.

If running isn't your thing, try walking, swimming, mountain biking or anything that gets you your 30 minutes of exercise each day.

You must do 30 minutes of exercise per day. *Make it a habit!*

Another thing you can do to slow down your mind is to take things one day at a time. Don't think too far ahead. It is very important that you prioritise your tasks and complete them in a timely manner before taking on more.

Step 10 summary

Celebrate your sales results and success. Discussing success can bring more.

A word on time management. Your time available to conduct face-to-face sales calls is limited; use it effectively.

Be a hunter and a farmer. Combine these two roles and you will be an awesome salesperson.

Know yourself. Understand yourself, including your strengths and weaknesses.

Sales conferences. Learn, have fun and always be on time in the morning! Look after your wingman.

Presentations. Prepare, plan and practice. Consider joining a Toastmasters group.

Mental health and exercise. Exercise a minimum of 30 minutes a day and make healthy eating choices.

What you've learned

As I've taken you through the ten steps that make up *The Knack of Selling,* you've learned about the following.

How to *prepare and plan* for a sales call. By taking action and applying what you learned in this step, you will be more organised and less nervous, and your behaviours will be more professional.

Think about painting: the preparation and planning that has to go into this task takes a lot of time. You need to organise all the paint and equipment, then prepare the surface to a high standard to achieve a fantastic end result. The preparation and planning is paramount to achieving the perfect result.

How to *practise* for a sales call. By taking action and applying what you learned in this step, you will master your sales call before even doing it. Your confidence will increase and your fears will be reduced.

Think about golf (which I'm not very good at except on corporate days with a few beverages): the more you practice, the lower your handicap gets as your skills improve.

How to *make initial contact* to get in front of your customer. By taking action and applying what you learned in this step, your nervousness will lessen, you will be well prepared, and your sales calls will go smoothly towards the outcome of progressing further to an order or a follow-up.

Think about the time you had one of your first dates. You needed to be very confident, you needed to be able to handle rejection if it didn't go your way, and you needed to lock down a time and a place to meet. It was in this initial contact that your relationship started to develop.

The *crucial things to consider for your sales call*. By taking action and applying what you learned in this step, you will come to be seen as very organised and professional in the customer's eyes—a most important attribute to have.

In one scenario during my career, I advertised a job role and received a number of applications. After shortlisting down to two potential employees, here is what happened.

The first potential employee arrived five minutes before the scheduled time, was well presented and had a happy persona during the interview. Not only that, they had a list with them of questions they had prepared to ask their future employer.

The second potential employee arrived five minutes later than the scheduled time, was dressed very casually and seemed unhappy. Their mobile rang while they were in the interview.

Who do you think got the job?

How to *attend a physical sales call.* By taking action and applying what you learned in this step, you will appreciate the importance of building a relationship with the key people within your customers' businesses. You will also gain skills related to negotiation and margin calculation.

Picture this: you sit down with your bank manager to negotiate a deal on a new credit card. They make an offer to you based on your credit rating (risk analysis), and you ask them to give you a bit of a discount on the interest rate and to waive the annual fee, as you have researched their competitors' offers. They give you a higher limit than you expected and a reduced rate, then offer you a brochure on credit-card insurance (the upsell) and put it in your hand, since in case you get into trouble, this will give you security. Most people will blow out their limit over time and the bank knows this thus making them more profit in the long run.

You can devise similar solutions for your clients to maximise the benefit for them, and the value for you, that comes out of every sale, and in doing so preserve some of your margin even in a spirited negotiation.

How to successfully *close the sale.* By taking action and applying what you learned in this step, you will always get an outcome from a sales call and never walk away with nothing. Mastering this will give you great confidence and satisfaction as you start to excel in your career as a sales representative.

Having no outcome from a sales call is like having a burger with no filling. It's a waste of everybody's time. This is the biggest single lesson you need to learn as a sales representative: make sure you get something to do as a result of your sales call. It could be an order, or just something to follow up. Communication with the customer must continue to flow for your relationship to develop.

Recently, at an event I attended, the presenter made a special offer to all in the audience that they could buy a product through their distributor. As a representative for just such a distributor, my mind instantly sensed the chance to get some sales. This was a new technology product that could be operated by voice control, and the presenter was passionate about the product taking off in the market. At the conclusion of the event, I networked the room and asked all attendees if they would like me to organise the special offer for them. I sold 10 packs, and meanwhile, my competitors had already left the building.

Don't wait for the sales opportunity to come to you; go to the opportunity and get the order!

How to *follow up with your customers.* By taking action and applying what you learned in this step, you will constantly be in contact with your customers, staying at the front of their mind and being likely to get more sales.

The sale is not done when it's done! After-sales service is as important as the sale itself, and may well result in another sale. It's all about communication.

How to *develop relationships with customers.* By taking action and applying what you learned in this step, you will secure ongoing business with your customers for years to come.

Think about this: over time, you can become the trusted advisor in your field of expertise. Better yet, your colleagues who are also specialists in their fields may also become part of your customers' networks of trusted advisors. Then, your business will be way ahead of the sales game and always at the forefront of your customers' minds. You will most likely be the first person they call for help with a problem, and after all, sales is all about solving problems.

How to *manage the business lifecycle*, bringing in new customers and staff as old ones depart or as your business grows. Mastering the shifts involved as businesses grow and decline will enable you to keep prospecting for more customers and build the business you are working for. This could create jobs for more people, and great satisfaction can come from this.

Think about this: sales representatives are employed to work mostly *on* the business, not *in* the business. If you don't adopt a mindset that lets you accommodate growing sales and the responsibilities that come with them, most of your time will eventually be spent working *in* the business, and eventually, the business will stop growing. That defeats the purpose of even having a sales representative.

How to *celebrate and work on yourself* once the selling is done. By taking action and applying what you have learned in this step, you will become a better person both mentally and physically. This will enable you to take leaps and bounds in your sales career, outshining those who have not followed the ten steps in *The Knack of Selling*.

Think about this: if you celebrate all your successful outcomes with the internal sales team and get them feeling the satisfaction you feel, you will give them the comfort that their job is secure because you are the head of sales and you are smashing it.

Keep in touch

You now have the tools you need to start selling or to sell more effectively, provided you are committed to *taking action*. As you can see from the above summary of the ten steps, *all of them require action from **you** if change is to happen*. The guarantee I can give you is that if you follow the steps and take the necessary actions, you will be successful.

I hope that I have helped you in some way, to add some skills or techniques to your everyday selling toolkit, or by giving you the confidence to apply for a sales position and hopefully start your career in sales.

Naturally, your journey doesn't end here.

My passion is sales, and you can only offer so much advice in a book.

I encourage you to keep in touch and to visit my website **knackofselling.com.au**. There you will find resources to keep you learning as you develop in your sales career. You can join the members' area where you can ask questions of myself and others who are in various sales roles, and view training videos that expand on topics discussed in this book. I can also be engaged to present at your next national conference or sales meeting.

So, please refer my book and website to any people within your business or industry who you think might also benefit from what you've learned here.

I would love to hear of your successes and how this book has helped you or someone you know. I also welcome any feedback, whether positive or negative. Write to me any time at sales@knackofselling.com.au.

Here's something to finish off with. Recently, in a coffee shop, I noticed this written on the wall:

Few things require zero talent:

Being on time
Work ethic
Effort
Body language
Attitude
Passion
Energy
Doing extra
Being prepared
Dressing up

How true! If you can bring these virtues into your everyday life, not only will you be successful in selling, but you will be happy and make others happy too.

Try it. You have nothing to lose!

Thank you for reading, I hope someday we may have a chance to meet in person, so you can tell me your stories of success from learning the ten steps that are *The Knack of Selling*.

WHAT'S NEXT?

In *The Knack of Selling*, I've taken you on an educational journey into the world of face-to-face selling.

The business world is full of salespeople. This book can teach you how to stand out from the crowd, but it requires *action* on your behalf to get the desired outcome and become the best possible salesperson you can be.

On my website, **knackofselling.com.au**, you can find further guidance in the members' area on how to put the ten steps you've learned about here into practice.

Your small investment in my book, together with the training videos available on my site, will mean bigger sales results for you. There is no reason you can't improve on who you are today, increase your confidence, remove your fears and get the tools to be successful.

Invest in yourself today and become the best salesperson you can be.

Step 6: Closing the sale

1. Mitsubishi, "2019 Hybrid SUV | Outlander PHEV – New Cars – Mitsubishi Motors," http://archive.is/AtbdX, accessed 8 July 2019.